Why am I F'd up?

a spiritual guide to understanding
the chaos in your life

Pamela Beaty

Acknowledgements:

To Dr. Mona Roy for her encouragement and steadfast support for everything I do.

To Jackie Morris, Susan Somers, Marcus Hunt and Joyce Campbell for their continuous friendship and love since the day we met.

To my clients over the past 18 years, without whom I would never have learned all the lessons in this book.

Table of Contents

Chapter One:	Human nature	13
Chapter Two:	God	24
Chapter Three:	Religion	32
Chapter Four:	Sex	42
Chapter Five:	Love	58
Chapter Six:	Pain is an opportunity	69
Chapter Seven:	Inner child	82
Chapter Eight:	Your subconscious mind: your protector	97
Chapter Nine:	Thoughts are things	108
Chapter Ten:	Ignorance is not bliss	121
Chapter Eleven:	Past lives and karma	127
Chapter Twelve:	Group consciousness	135
Chapter Thirteen:	Spirits and demons	142
Chapter Fourteen:	Spiritual growth ain't easy	152
Chapter Fifteen:	Get in the game	157
Chapter Sixteen:	Conclusion	163
Chapter Seventeen:	My story	167

Introduction

I'm sure you're wondering why a spiritual book would have a title that contains *the* ultimate curse word. I first came up with it because my clients were always saying it to me during their sessions: "Pamela, why am I so f'd up?" Their lives were a mess and they didn't understand why, so after fifteen years of hearing the same thing I decided that I would write a book about it. Plus I think the title is simple, straightforward, and it will stick out like a sore thumb in the bookstore. After all, what better way to get you to notice my book than to use a word that some consider an adjective while others consider it offensive? That word represents what has been considered a *bad* word in our society. According to my very religious family, a good person would never use that word. I'm a good person and I use that word to ultimately identify something that needs improving, not as a dirty word. I don't like the word when it's used to describe a beautiful, wonderful experience of lovemaking; I think it works much better as an adjective.

Through years of working as an Empathic Intuitive, Spirit Medium and Past Life Therapist, I began discovering the reality behind the ostensible chaos of our world. Discovering the truth has helped me to cope with living in a world where rape, murder, war, theft, and dishonesty seem to run rampant. I have my own personal reasons for actually writing this book. For years, I searched for answers to why my life was f'd up and could not seem to find any information that explained it all to me. Then, after years of seeking, I discovered it all by myself. So, as the old saying goes, "When you learn, you teach." I wanted to write a definitive book that explained the real reason behind the suffering in the world and the different causes of pain in order to enable others to understand the seeming irrationality of it. After all, the more you understand the truth behind the suffering, the more you can shift that suffering. Knowledge is power. When you understand the real reasons behind the chaos you can eliminate some of the chaos.

For the past fifteen years as an Empathic Intuitive I've helped my clients figure out why they were so f'd up. I helped them understand the real reasons behind their self-destructive behavior. By intuitively speaking with their internal energy systems and talking to their conscious, subconscious and higher conscious minds, I was able to help them know the truth about the thoughts that were causing them to be stuck in chaos.

Everyone experiences physical, emotional and mental pain at some time in his or her life. My goal is to give you the tools necessary to change your life from being an unhappy experience to a joyful one. Once you understand the reasons behind self-destructive behaviors, you can forgive yourself and once you forgive yourself you can heal. The understanding removes judgment, which is what causes you to stay in detrimental cycles of behavior in the first place.

The key to finding peace in the chaos is to understand the spiritual purpose for coming into a physical body in the first place. The reality is that you were created for one purpose only, to understand and discover yourself emotionally. Living in the chaos fulfills the need for emotional growth, as the chaos is an opportunity to grow through your unresolved emotions, thereby giving you spiritual knowledge. Your soul comes from pure love and its purpose is to return to pure love. It is innate, and from your first incarnation, it has been the driving force in your life: not money, not power, and certainly not success.

Everyone has problems. My intention is to help those who seek the answers to them, no matter their level of spiritual awareness. It's interesting when someone says they're on a spiritual path, because to me if you're breathing, you're on a spiritual path. The most evil human being alive is on a spiritual path – just not a very good one. Like decent human beings, they are struggling to learn to love themselves and others. But unlike the virtuous others, malevolent individuals aren't able to get past their own internal pain to discover the love within. There are those among us who would say I'm crazy to suggest someone like Charles Manson is on a spiritual path. The reality is someone like that has shut off all love from the inside, but when they incarnate it means they are trying to find it, which is a spiritual path. They do it because it's too painful to live any other way and their mantra becomes "hurt someone else before they hurt you." A spiritual path is one in which you experience pain, grow from that pain, and share the knowledge you gain from that pain. Who doesn't do that? Even though Manson is a despicable human being, his darkness clearly shows the rest of us what a void of love looks like. You can't know who you are until you know who you're not. His spiritual path was to show us how *not* to live our lives.

This book will not change the world *per se*, or turn evil beings into saints, but hopefully it will change individuals so individuals can save the world. Only when you find peace individually can you achieve peace as a totality.

This book will explain how to achieve peace by understanding the reasons and contributing factors to why you're f'd up. It will help you move out of the darkness of the question and into the light of the answer. There is a divine method to the madness of the illusion on this plane of existence commonly called *life* and once you understand it, your *life* will never be the same.

1
HUMAN NATURE

My grandmother had a saying whenever people screwed up: "That's being a human being; I'm so glad I'm not one of them." Trying to understand the actions of human beings is like a fourth-grader trying to understand astrophysics. We're a collective oxymoron that's often running to stand still; yet if we did stand still, we'd find there was no need to run. As human beings we devote a lot of time and energy to our mental and physical dysfunctions. We go to psychotherapists to help us understand our mental dysfunctions, physicians for our physical ailments, and religion to find ourselves spiritually. We've become so sophisticated as far as the medical profession is concerned; we've found cures for many diseases and are close to finding cures for others. We have the best medical care money can buy, but if working on the external, physical self was the answer, we'd all be living in utopia and perfect health. We have all this genius technology – yet we're more screwed up than we've ever been.

My fellow human beings fascinate me because of what they have made their life priorities. They'd rather be up to their asses in debt so their friends, co-workers, neighbors, and strangers on the street will be impressed, than go to sleep happy every night. They'll spend a full year's salary on a shiny new car, yet won't spend a dime on the soul driving it. They'll go to the gym, get manicures, spray tans, and designer clothes so everything looks perfect; but on the inside they're still weak, pale, and naked and they spend absolutely no time at all finding out why. There is nothing wrong with spending money on luxuries, but there has to be a balance to those priorities. What's more important: to look good or to feel joyous? It's a choice of how you spend your hard-earned money, but the interesting thing is that if you put healing your soul at the top of the list you could have it all. When you work on your soul, you have the potential to have all the things you want, look good, *and* be happy.

So there you are, looking good, feeling horrible, and pointing the finger at everyone else for your problems. Human nature has you being a victim and never taking responsibility for your own actions or life. Human nature has you blaming others for your lot in life instead of looking in the mirror. You've perfected judging others instead of looking at yourself. Human nature dictates that you judge others. Human nature dictates that you judge you. Human nature can be a real bitch.

Human beings have become collectively more narcissistic and fearful. As long as you get your way, no one else really matters. You do whatever it takes, which includes creating boundaries. Human nature says that you protect yourself at all costs. After being hurt in your childhood, you start drawing lines in the sand and daring anyone to cross. The problem is that the internal boundaries you create are based on the fear of what happens if someone does cross those lines. If you love yourself enough and are living a joyful, centered life, you will not need to establish boundaries because there is nothing to fear. If you love yourself enough, you will not manifest anyone in your life that would overstep your internal boundaries. You will have no need for that drama; you will have no need for that lesson because you've made peace from within.

On the surface, the physical world seems so complicated. On the surface, it looks like humans are a deplorably selfish and doomed species. On the surface, it looks like the world is flawed to the point of no return. On the surface, it looks like the whole planet is f'd up and needs to call it a day. But gold was never buried on the surface. You have to dig deeper. If you believe that human beings are all formed from the same glorious cloth of a divine being, then you must also believe there is a really good reason they are f'd up. If you sit back and truly become aware of human nature, without judging human nature, you will become aware of the truth of what you see. If you look at the world as anything but divine inspiration, you will have the propensity to feel defeated, disgusted, and unhappy; but if you change your perspective of the world to what it really is – a controllable illusion – the chaos dissipates and it will be impossible to feel anything but confidence, acceptance, and joy.

As a human being you are desperate to control your external world because it feels like your external world is controlling you. You fight with your neighbors, family, lovers, associates, and strangers; anyone you feel is keeping you from having control. The reality is that *you* are the one responsible for the lack of control and your ego demands you fight the good fight in order to be in control, to be right. But here's the secret – there is no right and wrong. Right and wrong are usually determined by time and geography. What was right in the fifties – men bringing home the bacon and women frying it up in the pan – is wrong today. What was right in ancient Rome – people being publicly crucified for opposing the Emperor – is wrong today. There is no right and wrong in the eyes of God either. God doesn't have a scoreboard or cheerleaders who raise their pompoms when someone is declared the winner. Your ego is the one keeping score. Your ego feels better when someone says you're right. When you learn that and let go of the ego's need to be right, you have control of your internal world, removing the need to fight and control your external world. The only real control you have in the world is how you feel about it.

As you fight with others, you stumble into the negative need for apologies. As a human, you crave them, certain the only way the wrongs will be righted is if the wrongdoer apologizes to you. As long as you have that need, you will continue to manifest reasons for the apologies; you will continue to manifest others *wronging* you; you will continually perpetuate manifesting negative needs. Once you change your internal feelings and relinquish the need to be right in every situation, you relinquish the need for apologies. The way to do that is to figure out what is right for *you* and you alone and to be comfortable in your own certainty of it without the need for someone to agree with you.

Have you ever ended a relationship without getting to say everything you wanted to say? Did you ever feel that burning sensation in your stomach that nothing would be right until you got closure? What does that mean? It means your ego is bruised. It means you didn't get to be right. It means you didn't get to prove to your lover that he or she wronged you and they are the one with the problem not you. You can never have closure with anyone else as long as you *need* to have it. Breakups are hard and filled with question marks, but if you focus on the gifts of the relationship rather than the suffering, you will be at peace with it. If you focus on what you learned about yourself in the relationship instead of being mad at yourself for being in the relationship, you won't need closure from the lost love because you will have found it within yourself.

It truly is always darkest before the dawn, so if the conditions of the world are indeed getting worse, that means it's about to get better. Human beings are learning at a faster pace than ever before. Thanks to technology, you know within minutes what's happening on the other side of the world and thanks to the media's propensity to focus on the negative aspects of human nature, you get the opportunity to see who you are *not* now more than ever. If viewed from the right *perspective* this can truly help you change the world by realizing who you should be. It's human nature to grow and now you have more opportunities than ever to do just that. Like technology, your learning curve is speeding up. As you continue the descent to rock bottom and awaken to what terrible really is, the transformation process can begin, which is what you truly desire.

As a group consciousness we realize that after all of our incarnations, we should have the knowledge we need by now. You want to grow, you want to change, and from a higher consciousness perspective, you realize that change is inevitable. You keep running into technical difficulties. You think your system is flawed yet you don't bother to check the manual, but if you did you'd see you don't need a whole new system; rather, you just need to better understand the system.

As I was doing a rewrite on this book, Barack Obama was elected the 44th President of the United States. To me, this is a sign that as a group consciousness we are choosing to change. As a group consciousness we are awakening to the truth. I wrote this in my blog last night.

> *It's midnight and I am still crying tears of joy. An indescribable peace permeates my soul. In the last election, when Bush stole – oops – won the*

election, I had almost given up hope for awareness. Watching our new president give his acceptance speech was one of the most touching, hopeful moments of my life. I had almost given up on our country to realize the truth and act upon it. I had almost given up hope that as a country and as a collective consciousness we would want to continue growing and learning. I had almost given up hope of having a truly undivided nation. Even though our founding fathers dictated a nation where all men (and women) are created equal, I had almost given up hope for that possibility.

The collective consciousness has chosen a path of change. There is a shift in consciousness! We have unequivocally stated we will no longer sit back and allow our politicians to take advantage of our complacency. We will no longer be complacent. We will no longer be distracted away from the actions of our leaders by the actions of celebrities. We will no longer pay more attention to what Jennifer Aniston does with her hair, with how "hot" Paris Hilton thinks she is, with whether or not Brad Pitt and Angelina Jolie are adopting or having another child or whether or not George Clooney is dating. We will no longer spend more time online reading TMZ or PerezHilton.com than we do reading Newsweek or the Economist. Politicians, we are awake and we are watching.

As I've stated before, we owe our awakening to the dysfunctional, disloyal, and downright narcissistic presidency of George W. Bush. His selfish, uncaring, entitled disposition almost cost us our country. By voting for Barack Obama we are sending a message to politicians, that we will no longer tolerate inept, irresponsible, aggressive, unbending behavior.

This election has had a profound effect on my soul, as I am sure it has yours. Thanks to this election, I once again have hope for a positive, caring, united UNITED STATES OF AMERICA. HOPE WON!

Contrary to popular belief, human beings aren't flawed; they only perceive themselves to be. If you alter your perspective, you will realize you are not f'd up, but divinely crafted. You will realize there is a reason behind your seemingly f'd up personality. When you change your perspective you will realize your flaws are simply opportunities for growth. Your lives are supposed to be filled with the good and the bad so that you are able to tell the difference. A negative, f'd up experience opens the door for a positive emotional outcome. In the moment you won't feel good about it, but after you have survived it, you will. That is the whole point of life, to survive and feel good afterwards. When you survive a f'd up situation you feel better about yourself for surviving it. You feel proud that you could triumph over the obstacle. You came, you saw, you kicked butt! When you change your perspective, you release the negative cellular memory from your soul and you grow spiritually because of it. Cellular memory is the hypothesis that memories, habits, interests, and tastes are stored in all the cells of your body and brain. Your soul remembers everything that has ever happened to it until the time you resolve the emotions, or karma, relating to those memories. Cellular memory is a vehicle for your karma in this lifetime. Your cells remember so that you can resolve the karma and move on spiritually.

The following human characteristics were divinely designed for the purpose of spiritual growth.

Human flaws

— Denial

It's so easy to ignore your own tendencies in life. Looking at the bad stuff about yourself is scary because of your high expectations. You wholeheartedly believe in perfection and are taught to strive for it and that belief keeps you in denial. You simply can't handle being imperfect. You think it's a bad thing when it isn't; yet when you stop denying you have issues, you will start having fewer issues. You just have to be ready to do it. The purpose of denial is to protect your loving spirit until you're truly ready to see negative aspects of yourself, no matter how much your friends and families can see self-destructive behavior. Until you're ready to acknowledge it, you won't be ready to change it, so denial is a source of protection of your sensitive souls.

— Seeing the worst in others

Human nature has you looking for the worst in almost everybody, unless, of course, you're physically attracted to them, in which case you sometimes ignore all the negative traits. How can being so critical of others be part of the divine plan? It's simple. You were programmed for growth, so by judging everyone else's issues you eventually realize they are really your issues. You manifest into your life other human beings that have the same negative qualities that you do. You manifest mirrors of your own flaws so that you can be made aware of them and then be given the opportunity to change them. Then bingo! growth happens.

— Lack of compassion

You view the flaws in others with tremendous judgment and don't take the time to realize they're suffering too.

More often than not you fail to feel compassion for your fellow human beings' problems. The gift in this is that being compassionless forces your soul to focus on yourself. You focus on yourself until you are at an awareness level where you realize when you don't feel compassion for others you are not capable of feeling compassion for yourself. Humans are all on different levels of spiritual awareness. You can't be where you're going until you're there, and you have to accept that not everyone is going to get it at the same time as you are. There are levels of *getting it* and being compassionless is just one of them. The less compassionate ones will come around when they're ready. Are you ready?

— *Poor me*

How many times have you sat around boo-hooing about your horrible life? How many pity-parties have you hosted? You were intended to experience self-pity. Self-pity is a motivator, as people will eventually feel so sorry for themselves that they get tired of it and become motivated to change. You will continue to make excuses for yourself until you're bored with the sound of your own pitiful story and will then take action. When you do that, you experience growth euphoria.

— *Self-defecating*

Yes, you read that correctly. Nag, nag, nag, that's all you do. You heap dirty, nasty complaints on yourself, day in and day out and when you're finished doing it to yourself, you do it to anyone in your path. You pile on the crap. You're so good at it that it's become an art form. How in the world can that be helpful? Well, you were created and incarnated for the purpose of better understanding yourself. When you self-defecate, you hear yourself talking about all the behaviors of someone you are *not* and in the process, you learn to understand yourself. Eventually you will tire of nagging yourself for what you are not and praise yourself for what you've discovered you are. You will change, and change is a good thing!

— *Self-absorbed*

In the past, being self-absorbed was the way of the world; however, due to recent celebrities making charity "cool", people are slowly starting to change. It's now in vogue to give to those less fortunate than us. It's cool to buy a red t-shirt that says, "INSPIRED." Being self-absorbed was designed to force you to look out for your own needs and help you realize you're important too. Slowly our society is becoming self-aware instead of being self-absorbed. Onward and upward!

— *Unaware*

At your creation, you were given the divine right to grow at your own pace. Being deliberately unaware allows you to change and grow at your intended pace with individuality and originality in order to discover the specialness of your individual soul.

All of these human characteristics are part of the celestial strategy for growth without judgment. They are human nature because they are all traits of God. In the next chapter, I'll discuss the true nature of God. No one wants to believe that God created negative emotions, but God is everything, and that includes being aware that you'll get it whenever you're ready to get it. It doesn't matter how you come into the world, it only matters how you go out. You have an innate desire to remember your divinity and your human flaws help you to do it; they help you along the road to awareness. You can drive as slow or as fast as you want along that road; you can take the scenic route or the freeway and you'll still get there. Human nature can be rewarding if you stop to understand it. You think you're so complicated, but you are all really quite simple. You all have the same opportunities, emotions and fears; they just present themselves in different scenarios and it's up to you to define your perspective of those scenarios.

The truth is that everything that is happening in your life, be it good or bad, has to do with the growth of your soul. Human nature is divine. There is a reason for everything you do, every thought you have, and every event you manifest. Every human being was dissected and understood *before* they were spawned. God played out every scenario before dividing and creating us. God knows the reasons behind your actions in this experiment of life. You're a game and you'll never understand the spiritual game until you play it. So, get in the game and take the time to understand your Creator's perspective; by understanding God you will understand the reason why you're f'd up.

2
GOD

Who or what is God and what does God look like? I bet you're asking yourself what on earth does a book on being f'd up have to do with God? The reason I wanted to include a chapter on God in this book is because I believe that mankind's philosophy of God is part of the root cause of being f'd up.

My childhood experience, as a member of the Missionary Baptist Church, taught me that God made man in his own image, so naturally I thought God looked just like a man. He/she doesn't. God is not anthropomorphic. God is not a man with long white hair and a beard. God is energy and each of us is a manifestation of that energy, an individualization of God. Each of us has our own unique spark of God. God is a belief system. God is all around and inside of us. God is everything. What God is *not* is a church with rules. Civilization has its rules, not God. Civilizations and cultures create rules about God, but those are not of God. Churches try to dictate how you live your life, not

God. Right and wrong is man-made, not God-made. God made all of creation and creation itself.

What is the real reason that God created this planet? What is the real purpose behind the creation of this f'd up planet? How did this happen? How did we all get here and how did we get so f'd up in the first place? Who is our creator and wouldn't you like to know what he/she was thinking when he/she created this planet? If there is a Hell, is this it? Why would a creator filled with divine knowledge and love create this Hell we live in? How can God, or whomever you believe created this planet, sit back and watch the chaos and not react? How is it possible that a creator of love could create such a f'd up place? How can God sit back and watch us continually screw up and not intervene? How could God sit and watch 9/11 happen and not punish those murderers? These are questions that need to be answered. I can answer them all with one word: perspective. Perspective is the reason that our creator does not step in and save or destroy this f'd up mess of a place we live in. Perspective.

To better explain God's perspective, I should first give you mine. I believe that in the beginning God was just one whole being filled with love and perfection. He/she/it was hanging out thinking, "Damn, I'm good. I'm the ideal. I am perfection. I am love." Then God wondered, "How do I know that? How do I know I'm so great? How do I know that I am perfect when I don't know what imperfect is? I can't possibly understand who I am until I know who I am not." God wanted to really know what love was by knowing what love wasn't. God loved *feeling* so much that God decided to divide and conquer, so God split up into millions of little emotional pieces and in that moment, creation, or what scientists like to call "The Big Bang" happened.

You are a piece of those pieces of the divine. You are here because of God, because you are a part of God. You're here because you're a part of a holographic Universe where every piece of the shattered glass of the Universe contains the entire Universe. You're here and continue to stay here because parts of your soul have come to the realization of your divine association and parts have not. You continue to return to this emotional theme park in order to feel the opposite of your origin so you can appreciate your origin. It's all a game. The game is to get as many pieces of your perfection as possible while you're on this game board called Planet Earth. Your mission, should you choose to accept it, is to figure yourself out. Figure out all you can about yourself. What makes you tick? What makes you sad, happy, angry, fearful, jealous, envious, greedy, or joyous? You can't discover yourself by running from yourself. Self-discovery is why you're on Planet Earth; just like God. So stop judging yourself and instead discover yourself, because only then can you stop being f'd up and return to the true divine God.

Several years ago I was in a difficult emotional time in life. I was horribly depressed with the state of the world. Then, as now, mankind was cruel to one another. There was fighting in the streets and homes, murder, famine, rape, road rage, theft, and suicide bombings in the name of Allah. In order to cope with it, I would spend one Sunday a month at home alone, crying my eyes out, having what I called, "Nervous Breakdown Sunday." I literally had a broken heart from what I thought was an injustice to God. I would sob uncontrollably as my body shook releasing the pain. After several months of this I started talking to God about it and in the middle of apologizing on behalf of my fellow humans, I heard a burst of joyous laughter. I ran through my house, trying to find who was there. I was alone. The laughter continued and then was joined by *The Voice*.

"Let me ask you a question," said The Voice. "When you feel my presence, does it feel like I'm in pain to you?"

to me, I replied, "No, all I feel is the love."

The Voice said, "Well then, I guess what's happening doesn't hurt me."

"Then why does it hurt me?" I asked.

God replied: "Because you judge it."

That stopped me dead in my tracks. I thought I was the least judgmental person on the planet. How could I be judging people? Apparently that was indeed what I was doing.

So, I asked God, "Why do I judge what is happening in the world?"

"Because you don't know enough. If you understood the reality of your world you would rejoice in the status, not be saddened by it."

I found out that day that I was not only a judgmental ass, but also that I didn't know squat about life. Ouch. From that day forward I never needed another Nervous Breakdown Sunday.

Once I stopped judging and began accepting, I stopped struggling emotionally. Notice I said, "I stopped struggling"; I didn't say I stopped experiencing pain. I still experience pain and the opportunities for growth that accompany it. I just choose not to suffer with it. God understands that even if it's bad here, it's good here. God's perspective is that there are no mistakes. Each and every thing that happens, be it good or bad, is just another opportunity to understand how perfect you and God are. You can't make a mistake in God's eyes. This concept might piss off a few people because they think that God should judge bad people; however, God judges no one! A true and perfect God could not make any mistakes and as you are a part of God, neither can you. Your ostensible mistakes are just opportunities to understand yourself better and when you understand yourself better, God is happy because God has an emotional experience.

I recently treated a young mother with cancer. During one of the sessions I felt a tremendous amount of guilt in her soul. I told her I felt she was feeling guilty because she had negative, fearful thoughts about her disease. She was terrified that by *thinking* she might die she was going to cause herself to become sicker. She felt guilty because she had days where she just wanted to cry about her disease and the prospect of leaving her young child motherless. She told me that every time she feels sad or scared, her friends tell her that she has to have more faith in God and if she's scared it means she doesn't have enough faith. Unfortunately, this is very common. People tend to push this unrealistic, untruthful crap on unsuspecting innocent people all the time. The idea that she doesn't have faith because she gets scared and has negative thoughts is contrary to the whole point of our existence - to feel. No wonder she's so upset. How could she not be with all the pressure to be perfect?

God does not punish people by making them sick and then punish them further by making them sicker if they don't have enough *faith*. God is an omniscient, all loving being that understands every emotion or thought you have, be it positive or negative. You are made in the image of God, so God had to have felt everything *before* you did. You have those negative emotions because God had them first. You were created with the propensity to feel and feel everything. Your feelings are innate and your source of integrity, they are your inner compass. You can trust your feelings well before you can trust your thoughts. Your mind has an agenda; your feelings are your truth.

Let your feelings out. You are not offending God by being afraid, you are honoring God by being afraid. You are not pissing God off when you get angry; you are expressing God when you feel angry. God is *every* emotion. In God's eyes it doesn't matter what you feel as long as you *feel* something. God rejoices when you feel something and express it. You

Trying to be cool, controlled, and unfeeling for the sake of God doesn't work. You're in denial of God when you hold back your emotions, be they love, anger, sadness, disappointment, or guilt. God benefits from you expressing them all. Expressing emotions is God-like, so stop judging yourself for being God-like. Go ahead and cry, get angry, be scared or sad, because once you feel the emotions, express them, and release them, you can figure out what caused them later. You can be the objective observer of your own emotions. Being the objective observer is what brings about healing. If you continue to judge, you will continue to be f'd up.

Several years ago Don Miguel Ruiz published an amazing book called *The Four Agreements*. In it he stated, "Hell is a state of mind." Hell is in our own minds. There is not a physical place of existence that is Hell. Hell is what we think. If you think your life is a living Hell, it is. I bring this up now because I'm talking about creation and how you were designed. You were designed in the image of God, the ultimate thinker. God created this opportunity to discover the ultimate truth of who you are, so take advantage of it. You've spent most of this life finding out who you aren't; don't you think it's about time to find out who you are? You are a replica of God, no matter who you are or what you've done; you are the spitting image of God. You, like God, are on a journey of self-discovery. You, like God, get to choose what that journey is like. You, like God, can be good or bad. You, like God, can be in Hell. You, like God, have a *get out of Hell free card*. It's called *choices*. If you don't like your life, you can choose a new one. The choice is your thoughts. You can move out of Hell into heaven on earth by just knowing that they are all a state of mind. Thank you, Don Miguel. *The Four Agreements* is recommended reading. It'll only take about one evening and it will change your life.

At different times in your life, and for some, their entire lives, it's difficult to believe in God or any all-powerful force, especially when it comes to asking for things and then not receiving them. You get angry and upset when what you think you need and want doesn't manifest. Yet, you need to remember that often, after a short period of time, something much better comes along, and with it comes the realization that the original thing may actually have harmed you in some way. Garth Brooks' song *Thank God for Unanswered Prayers* expresses this concept extremely well. He wrote that song because the girl he loved in high school rejected him and because of that rejection, he ended up finding his wife and the mother of his children.

You pray for things you *think* you need and when they don't manifest you stop believing in God, but God has a much better viewpoint of your life than you do. God knows there's something better just around the corner and it's better than what you could ever imagine. It may seem that your prayers are going unanswered, but in reality, he's/she's giving us the better answer. When you're praying, you just need to remember that. Instead of praying to God for something you want, visualize what you want. *See it*. Then thank God for creating it. Instead of begging God for something, imagine you already have it. Imagining and believing are the two prayers that work.

Inspiration

When you pray to God to give you what you want you are using your limited consciousness and will power instead of remembering that God *knows* what is best for you. You just need to feel love and joy in your heart, focus on the things that make you feel good, get out of the way and let God take care of the rest. Be happy and that happiness will create those things that will make your life joyous. Once you focus on happiness, rather than sadness and frustration, an idea or thought will magically pop into your head. When you get that inspired thought, take immediate action and do something with it. You can't create anything unless you are first inspired to do it and then do something with that inspiration. Creation is about inspiration and perspiration. That's the same way everything in your world was created. Once you embrace that, you will find your inspired actions are effortless, as opposed to actions out of desperation and frustration, which often feels like you're banging your head against a brick wall. You can *feel* the difference. When you aren't inspired you work twice as hard and get half the results. When you're inspired, things just fall into place.

Inspiration + Perspiration = *Creation.*
Creation is God.

Most people believe more in their religion or church than they believe in God. They worship the idol instead of the ideal. They believe what their ministers, priests or rabbis tell them to believe. In my humble opinion, religious dogma causes more people to be f'd up than any other single transgressor on this planet. So, I had to include a chapter on religion in this book. I'm certain that what I have to say will not be well received by any religious group. But it doesn't matter because the title of my book alone will be enough to piss them off, so what I say about their religious beliefs will almost be a moot point. If you are an avid church-going religious person, you may not like what you read, but as I respect your right to believe as you wish, I ask humbly for you to respect my belief.

3
RELIGION

As I stated in the last chapter, there are aspects of religion that can cause you to be f'd up. My feelings are based on my personal life and the experiences of being a preacher's kid as well as my common sense approach to comprehending religion. As the daughter of a Baptist minister, I understand all too well what happens when the Bible is used as a weapon for control. My father certainly used the Bible as a weapon against my sisters and I. He interpreted it to say that God only spoke to male ministers; God punished sinners with eternal life (*after* death) in a fiery furnace; God judged and punished us if we dared to make a mistake; and that anyone other than saved members of the Missionary Baptist Church were going to Hell. I was even told that once you were *saved* you could sin but still get into the pearly gates. God would be really pissed at you, but once you were forgiven you would be welcomed into the heaven of Missionary Baptists. Does that sound logical?

When I was twelve years old I was told I was a sinner and unless I was saved I would be doomed to an eternity in a fiery furnace. How could anyone with common sense believe that a twelve year old could have done something so wrong that she would be doomed to Hell? They believed it because they were told to believe it. This unfathomable idea was handed down from generation to generation and each generation was afraid *not* to believe it.

Naturally, as a curious child, I had some questions about my family's religious beliefs. I once asked my grandmother, a minister wannabe, why God would condemn a really good person to an eternity in a fiery furnace just because they weren't part of our church or had been saved by our church. Her answer was that God would make certain that everyone had an opportunity to be exposed to a Missionary Baptist Church and they had to make a choice whether to be saved or not. I asked her how that was possible and she told me, "Because it says so in the Bible." In all my years of studying the Bible, I never once saw that canned response, so I knew that it could not be true. I knew that it wasn't written anywhere in the Bible that only Missionary Baptists were going to heaven. Later, I realized that all religions have some variation of that "Go with us or go to Hell" philosophy. I also realized that I had to be an independent thinker and find out what God meant to me, not what it meant to me via my parents and their church.

What made it difficult for me to have my own opinions about God and the Bible was a personal experience I had while attending church. Like so many other churches, my family's church had numerous revivals every year. During these revivals, lost souls were supposed to pray to God for the purpose of being saved. Children of all ages would beg God for forgiveness. They would pray at the altar for hours for instructions from God as to what He wanted them to do in order to guarantee that their souls would be saved from an eternity in a fiery furnace. During one of these revivals, I was the one sitting at the altar praying to God to save my soul. I was terrified that I would die before I was saved and if I did I was indeed doomed to Hell. I was even afraid of climbing trees because I might fall and die! I was terrified of riding in a car, walking down the street, or going anywhere because I was so afraid that my life would be taken before I was saved. It really was one of the scariest times of my life.

One night, while at the altar praying, I heard a thought in my head that said I should get everyone to sing the classic Baptist song, "Ole time religion." My grandmother was kneeling and praying beside me, so I told her I wanted to sing that song. She told the rest of the congregation that I wanted to sing that song, so they did. During that rendition, I had a feeling that could only be described as euphoric. I felt the most glorious feeling of light and love surge through my body. It felt as if I were soaring through the heavens straight to God. The feelings were indescribable. I was filled with the most incredible joy. I could not stop laughing – I had been saved! From that point on, I was free to climb trees, ride in cars, walk down the street, and go wherever I wanted to go; I was fearless.

What was really confusing about that night was those feelings. Years after, when I became a seeker of truth instead of a robot of dogma, I could not understand how my family's beliefs about God could have been so wrong, yet I was able to have those euphoric feelings. That confusion kept me from totally becoming engulfed in a different way of thinking. With the help of meditation, various visions of God, and being able to replicate those euphoric feelings, I was able to transcend those fears and embrace my own philosophy.

When I decided to include a chapter on religion in this book I had to decide how I wanted to go about convincing you that the Bible, the Koran, or any other book on religion was written and invented by man. In convincing you that your fear-based religious views are harmful to your soul, I did not want to be hypocritical. Each religion believes their religion is the only truth. I truly want people to believe what they feel is right for them. Yet, I truly want people to be free of the fear that most religions put upon them. I just want to express my experiences and allow you to come to your own conclusion.

I did some research on the history of the Bible to be able to ascertain who really wrote it. I wanted to write facts in order to convince you of my belief, but I decided that if I did that, I would be no different than any other religious organization in trying to convince you that my version of the truth was the truth. Hundreds of books have been written against the religious dogmatic principles of the Bible, which used facts and explanations that should make people realize that the Bible is a storybook, yet people still devote their lives to the "Good Book." Instead of trying to convince you that my interpretation of the Bible is the true interpretation, I decided instead to appeal to your common sense. Hopefully when you really take the time to analyze the Bible stories for believability you will be able to realize the truth.

Just like politics, religion has different perspectives. Since the Bible was written, rewritten, and translated by various groups, its natural parts would have been misinterpreted and changed throughout history. It was written in three languages and transcribed into many others. Transcription is in and of itself susceptible to mistakes. But the single most important reason to question the validity of the Bible document is that you *do not know who wrote it*. Why should I believe something written by someone who I have no idea of their agenda? In my life, I am very careful about whose opinion I value. I do not choose to believe something unless it's experiential, yet the religious community wants me to live my life according to a book that was written thousands of years ago by people no one knows, transcribed from languages that could have been misconstrued by religious scholars, and then edited by editors with an agenda. I don't think so. My common sense will not allow this blind faith.

Although the Bible is a great storybook, I do not believe it is supposed to be taken literally. In order to maintain control, the early Catholic Church changed the good book to make it a story that would control people through fear. Many of the books of the original Bible were left out when it was determined they didn't fit into man's need for power over the people. Some were left out because they portrayed women as powerful leaders, and at the time, that was forbidden. For the most part, religious scholars cannot even agree what the Bible verses mean. Every religion on the planet interprets it in a way that fits nicely into what they want to believe. I know my family did that. They manipulated the words to justify their dogma, thereby making their religion the only true way to God and themselves the chosen ones.

Reasons to believe

In the Bible, God is a vengeful, angry, power-hungry jerk who insists on being worshipped and adored and if you don't, he'll get ya! He might kill you or, in Adam and Eve's case, curse you to a life of hard work. Then in Genesis 6:5–8 the Lord says, " I will blot out from the earth the human beings I have created – people together with animals and creeping things and birds of the air, for I am sorry that I have made them." So God sent a flood, and with the exception of Noah, his peeps and two-by-two animals, mankind was wiped out. This God guy is kind of an ass that you don't dare cross or basically it's either off with your head or drowning by flood.

In Sodom and Gomorrah God gets pissed, once again, with the so-called evil and sends down burning sulfur to wipe out the cities. Religions have used this story to justify punishing homosexuals. Does this really make sense? Why would an all-powerful force need to wipe out a village because people of the same sex are having sex? Why would the creator need to destroy what he created? If God were an all-knowing being, wouldn't he/she have anticipated the need for souls to have their own experience? After all, God IS the experience. So, God would have had no reason to destroy the earth; he would have seen the gay lifestyle coming. To me, that means he/she wasn't against it because he/she created it.

Why would a being that was capable of creating the heavens and the earth need to be worshipped and adored? If you were such a powerful being that you could create the heavens and the earth, would you really be so petty as to care not only that people were having sex, but also how they engaged in that sex? No, you wouldn't. God is not petty; people are petty.

My question to you is, why would you want to worship and obey such an ass? If God were vengeful enough to do some of the horrible things that are documented in the Bible, why would you worship him? Surely you wouldn't. How could you? God forbid you have a bad day or a weak moment because if you do, on a whim, God could destroy you. This is not the type of being I would respect, let alone worship.

All I know is that if the message of the Bible is not one of love and compassion for your fellow man or woman, if the message hurts anyone in any way, if the message judges anyone and determines right or wrong, then it is being misinterpreted. God does not judge. God does not determine right or wrong. God just loves, God just understands and accepts, therefore, we all should just love and accept our fellow human beings whether they agree with us or not.

What if God truly is a loving being that does not punish? What if Jesus was simply the best of mortal man and he was married? What if women have the right to speak with God as much as men? What if you could find God without going to church? What if God is not an anthropomorphic God, but a God of loving energy and divine knowledge? The worlds of all religions would be rocked. How could they control their congregations without the use of fear as a deterrent?

The reality is that everyone is capable of getting in touch with the God within themselves and discovering their truth. This fact terrifies religious groups, because it threatens their hold on mass consciousness. They do everything in their power to make you believe what they believe because their livelihood is dependent on it. There is a lot of money at stake in organized religion. Some religious organizations have even set up their charges to be dependent on their congregation for financial stability. The money that's needed for these organizations to be profitable would disappear if no one were attending church, so they use the fear that drives them to control their congregations. They need you more than you need them. Have you noticed the size of the Vatican? It looks like the Catholic Church is more than solvent, but what would happen if their congregation stopped donating?

For some people, churches can and do serve a good and higher purpose. I've met many devoted churchgoers that are living Christ's message of love, so I don't want to indicate in any way that I think all who attend church are misguided and wrong. If I did that, I would be no different or better than them. Churches can be a wonderful way to connect with God, to keep your life on track, and to discover your truth. Those churches come in all shapes and sizes and need not be large and ornate. In fact, according to Jesus, two or more people gathered in God's name is all you need. I do not attend any church, nor am I affiliated with any religious or spiritual organization. I get up every morning, meditate and read inspirational material. It reminds me of who I am and how I should live my life. That is my church. If going to a church gives you inspiration and makes you a more loving and caring person who lives your truth; that is what you should do. The choice is yours. It is when you start stepping on the choices of others that faith becomes a negative attribute. Everyone is entitled to worship God as they see fit, but they should just go through life being a living example of those values, and not try to push them on others. If you live your life as a good example of a religious person, you will inspire others to follow your lead.

You should all have faith in whatever you want as long as it does not impinge upon the rights of your opposition. If the religious practices of others make you unhappy, then something is wrong with you, not them. If you were a member of the Baptist Church, why would you care how Catholics worship God? Every religion wants to believe that their way is the only way into the Kingdom of Heaven, but asking someone else to put aside their beliefs because they are not the same as yours is hypocritical. You wouldn't do it; so why would you expect them to?

God does not show preferential treatment to anyone. No church, organization, or person has any better opportunity to get in touch with God than you do. Your devotion to discovering the God within is the only difference. Raising your consciousness to love is the path to God. Spread your joy, not your religion, regardless of which one you choose. If you feel you have a better shot at finding God through meditation, then meditate. If you feel your path is through a religious affiliation, be it Islam, Buddhism, Judaism, or Christianity, then go for it. If you live an exemplary life of loving kindness and compassion, you are God-like. Live your truth, but don't try to sell your truth to others. The price will never be right and they'll never view it the same way you do, because everyone has their own perspective.

Son of God

I would be remiss in discussing religion, creation and God, if I didn't mention Jesus Christ. I feel like the controversy surrounding Jesus is yet another reason our society is divided, which is another cause of the world being f'd up. It's so ironic that religious organizations *fight* over Christ, and the meaning of his life, something that was so contradictory to the preaching of Jesus. Jesus was not affiliated with any religious organization with the exception of his family upbringing as an Essene.

The mystery of his life will probably remain unsolved throughout eternity and all anyone can do is speculate because none of us were there. Those who disliked him, as well as those who claimed to love him, misunderstood him. The reason was because this divine messenger was just a mortal MAN, not a God. The reason he came as a mortal man and not as a holy ghost was that God wanted us to further learn and understand that you are of him and therefore capable of anything he is. Jesus was no more the Son of God than any of the rest of us, but he incarnated to bring us an incredible message: anything Jesus can do, you can do. Unfortunately, his message was misinterpreted so people elevated him to being the only God incarnate. Like the rest of us, Jesus was an individualization of God. Jesus was born of a woman and came to earth as a man to help us understand the innate God within us. He brought the message that nothing changes from outside of us and by raising your consciousness, you, and therefore God, heal from within.

Jesus came to redeem the entirety of the human race yet his message and life are still the source of controversy. Jesus spoke in parables so those who devoted the time to understanding his message would understand it and those who did not would seek to understand. He wrote in parables so that scholars would discuss and debate his message. Jesus wanted humans to discuss the meaning behind his message so they would be paying attention to his message. He understood the need for controversy and discussion and that is why he is considered to be the greatest spiritual teacher of mankind. His message was designed to make us seek the truth about ourselves. He knew that by seeking the truth about ourselves we would discover the God within.

Another controversial aspect of Jesus being sent as a mortal man is whether or not he was married. To religious scholars, this is a major issue, when it really shouldn't be. Jesus was an ordinary man, not a monk. He never declared his celibacy, nor did he mention that holy men should be celibate, so why would he not marry? Jesus' message was one of love, so doesn't it make sense that he would have wanted to physically express love and share his life with a partner? The masculine and feminine aspects of the soul were divinely designed to feel God when they unite, so why would the Son of God avoid it? Jesus' message was one of love and compassion, to help us understand that all men are aspects of God.

Religion is a tricky business. It is truly the source of some of the most f'd up philosophies of life, yet it is also the source of comfort for massive quantities of people. It is the source of contention among all people of our planet. There is no way that we will EVER all agree over God, Jesus, or the Bible. The best we can hope for is to not let our own beliefs f'up our lives or the lives of others. We can't let any book that was written centuries ago dictate how we treat each other. Love is the only religion and philosophy we should believe in.

4
SEX

My family raised me to believe that having sex was something you did only if you wanted to have children. My grandmother told me that sex was horrible and that I would hate it. She said that it was something women had to do to not only keep their man happy, but also so they could have kids. She told me that when I got married and my husband wanted to have sex I should just raise my nightgown and let him do his thing so I could get it over with. As you can imagine, with that kind of rave review, I was terrified of having sex. That was the extent of my sexual education. I know that those statements from my grandmother really f'd me up about my own sexuality. I know that the sexual abuse I experienced as a small child, as well as being raped, crippled my spirit from the moment of the first infraction. I was f'd up over sex for most of my life and I know I'm not alone, so I wanted to write a chapter on how, as a whole, society has a f'd up belief system about sex.

Sex was intended to be an absolutely beautiful excursion back to God. You have been falsely convinced that sex is something the body craves; the real reason behind the appetite for sex is the soul. It longs for a reconnection to your truth, but it can also cause harm to your soul if the physical hunger is because of a deeply buried wound. It can cause pain if the focus is strictly on fulfilling a physical need. More often than not, you are *not* fulfilling a physical need, but instead you are filling a hole in your soul. To heal you must be able to recognize the difference.

Men as well as women have holes in their souls that need filling. Men with low self-esteem need to have sex with as many women as possible. Women with low-self esteem must have sex with as many men as possible. Having many sexual partners strokes both men and women's egos. They both do it because they don't feel enough love for themselves and they *need* someone else to make them feel loved. They need someone to want them in order to feel valued.

In the last several years with sexually explicit movies and television, the exposure to sex has become more and more prevalent in our society, but that's not indicative of a healthy attitude or understanding about sex. Humans have a tendency to focus on the contemptible side of sex.

Sex and society

We live in a world that is bombarded by blatant sexuality; sex is everywhere. Unfortunately, most of it is contemptible and most of it is a diversion from love. Human beings have embraced porn as an acceptable form of expression of physical need. A very spiritual friend of mine once told me she watches porn because it helps her during masturbation; she claims that she needs it in order to feel that utopian feeling of the connection with God. She had convinced herself that the feelings of joy she got while having an orgasm justified watching porn. I explained to her that as long as she needed porn to feel God, she would never be able to feel God in any other way. Even though I believe sex is the way to feel the wonders of utopia, it doesn't end there. After you feel those feelings of joy during an orgasm, then you should follow it up with a meditation. That gives you an ideal opportunity to connect with the *one*.

Opinions over sex and sexual fantasies are about as diverse as can be. Religious fanatics try to make sex a moral issue; advertisers try to use it to sell everything from tires to toothpaste; attractive people are labeled as sexy, which ostensibly makes them more valuable; and strip clubs are some of the most profitable businesses in the world. Child pornography runs rampant on the Internet. On television and in movies young men and women parade around half naked to flaunt their physical bodies and their sexuality. Young female recording artists are forced to dress in skimpy clothing in order to sell more records. It's considered good business to prostitute young people in order to make money. Though they aren't selling their bodies for sex, they are selling their bodies to make money. The trashier the attire, the more record sales go up. Isn't that what prostitution is all about – selling your body? Yet prostitution is illegal in our country. Sexy bodies mean sexy profits. It has become standard behavior for young girls to dress in clothes that barely cover their bodies. A stand-up comedian recently said that with the trashy way women dress these days it's hard to tell the *working girls* (prostitutes) from the others.

Why are so-called sexy, attractive people deified? How does something that takes place behind closed doors saturate every aspect of our physical lives? What makes the sexual act a top priority in dating and relationships? How was it decided that you are supposed to have sex on the third date? Why do magazine covers feature sexy people on the cover and articles on how to be a good in bed? Contrary to popular belief, the existence of sexy people does not make the world a better place.

Looking good in clothes doesn't make you more consequential. Being sexy does not mean that you will do anything in your lifetime that helps to progress or enhance the value of the world, yet people seem to value the sexual attributes of men and women more than the actions of those individuals.

In this chapter I hope to show how the concepts and perspective about sex and sexuality can cause you to be f'd up. If you buy into the value society seems to put on sex, you would think that the only reason we exist is to have sex. If you buy into the hype, you'd be convinced that if you aren't sexy or aren't having sex on a regular basis that something is tragically wrong with you. The general consensus appears to be that if you have a good sex life you will have a good relationship. The consensus is wrong. Sex, good or bad, has nothing to do with a long-term happy relationship.

According to the belief of hundreds of my female clients, being good in bed or pretending to just love sex will not only catch a man but also keep him forever. They believe that the way to a man's heart is through his penis. On the other hand, men believe that a large penis will keep a woman at his beck and call. None of these sexual fantasies are true. I'll say it again; great sex has nothing to do with a long-term relationship. Long-term positive relationships are based on commonality, respect, caring, laughter, communication, integrity, honesty, and love. Relationships that are based solely on sex are not likely to last because they aren't about love and respect; instead they are based on bad karma. I'll explain bad karma and its connection to sex later on in this chapter.

A client of mine had a history of dating guy after guy, and falling deeply in love with each one of them. Each one was "the love of her life." After only a couple of dates, she swore that this man she barely knew was her soul mate so, of course, she had sex with them. She was deeply hurt when these relationships ended and could not understand why. I strongly suggested she stop having sex. She needed to stop and take a look at the reason she was falling in love with every guy she dated. Sex was just adding to her confusion about love. In that case, she's no different than a great deal of women; sex always confuses the issue of love. Her soul was using men to try to fill the void in her heart. Her father abandoned her as a child and her mother was an emotional wreck, so her soul was desperately trying to feel love. In her case, she needed to stop having sex because her inner child needed to feel loved. Her promiscuity was the direct result of her need to feel love. If you are using sex to fill the void in your heart, you need to stop having sex.

Even though sex can put us in touch with our divine truth, it's not enough. If sex is free of anxiety it has the power to transform us, but it rarely is. If sex is toxic, then the totality of life is screwed up. Sex is convoluted by karma. It's convoluted by unresolved emotions. If you take the karma and unresolved emotions out of the equation, you will indeed have an experience of pure, divine love.

With all this attention to something that brings just a few brief moments of euphoria, it made me want to investigate the reality of the purpose of sex. I believe in an all-knowing God, therefore I believe God did not make mistakes when he/she created this Universe, so even though it appears that the attitude about sex is one of the things that is f'd up about our planet, I know that's an illusion, so the obsession must be purposeful.

Divine purpose of sex

Your soul was created to incarnate, to gain emotional knowledge, through the experience of physical life. Sex is a part of that experience. In spite of evidence to the contrary the sexual deviancy in the world, the abundance of porn sites on the web, and sexual abuse sex was not designed to be a polluted act. Sex was divinely inspired to bring about the union of spirits. Sexual partners are able to have a transcendent experience by sharing themselves, body and soul. Sex takes you to a heightened awareness of your divine being. The indescribable feelings of an orgasm are the same utopian feelings of God. Sex fulfills the soul by replenishing the God within. Jesus said that you'd feel God's presence whenever two or more are gathered in his name; this includes the sexual experience. Sex is a way to remind you that we are all one. The euphoric feeling of an orgasm was created to remind you from whence you came.

Sex is the easiest way to communicate with God. Having that connection with the divine is one of the biggest motivators to have sex. Your soul hungers for that God union. Sex is never just about the physical experience; sex is about discovering your soul. With sex, more than any other modality, you can easily remember your divine love. You're attracted to another person because your soul recognizes their divine truth of love, and you long to feel true love, even if for only a few moments. The purpose of sexual fulfillment is to fill the void of the yearning for love from the very root of the soul. By using your body to feel the joy of love, you get connected to the oneness of consciousness. Sex reminds you of home.

It goes without saying that sex was also designed for reproductive purposes. It was deliberate that it feels good, thus encouraging humans to do it. In order for spiritual inhabitants to incarnate, we need bodies. You do what feels good and you create life – amazing!

Sex was also fashioned to be a tool for the ego. Sex is all about ego. Promiscuity is about ego and low self-esteem. Promiscuity is about your unhealthy, unhappy soul needing to feel loved. Experiencing multiple partners has nothing to do with loving sex; it's all about your ego. Anytime you're feeling unloved you will long for a sexual experience – not because you need the physical act, but because you need the love connection and because you need to feel valued. If you really just needed to have an orgasm you could take care of that all by yourself. The need for sex comes from the need for love. The more you *need* to have a partner, the more you *need* to spend time with yourself. Your ego needs you to tell it that you are loved; having another person tell you is a temporary fix. Having sex with a stranger, or someone you barely know is to satisfy your wounded soul. If you don't spend time learning to love yourself, you will always need that temporary fix.

Sexual experiences give your soul the opportunity for growth. When a sexual partner abandons you, you are forced to grow spiritually. When a sexual partner cheats on you, you are forced to grow spiritually. When someone you are attracted to rejects you, you are forced to grow spiritually. Basically, sex forces you to grow spiritually. It forces you to learn to love yourself. I know that anytime the vagina gets involved in a relationship, there is opportunity for growth. Women are all about intimacy, and having sex is the ultimate form of intimacy to women. When you have an amazing sexual experience with a man, it is more often related to karma than love.

Karma and sex

Anytime you have an uncontrollable need to have sex with someone you barely know, you're dealing with karma. If you meet someone and are instantly attracted to him or her, you are dealing with karma. If all you can think about is sex with this new person, you are having a karmic reaction. Whenever there is a negative karmic relationship your ego will have a need to connect, not only spiritually but also sexually. Your soul knows no space and time, so if it feels unloved by someone in a past life, it will continue to feel unloved by that person until it heals the pain. Your soul needs to resolve those wounds so it will have an innate need to have sex. It erroneously believes that the connection to God during sex will cause the other person to fall in love with you.

The more passionate you feel for someone you have just met, the more you can be assured that you have a deep karmic connection. Your soul is designed to heal; it innately believes that connecting physically will help it to do just that. Your ego desires to heal this negative karmic relationship so it convinces you that you desire sex. Sex isn't the goal; healing is the goal, but your subconscious feels that sex is a tool to healing. It isn't. The tool to healing is self-love and self-love only. You never need to have the love from another to heal; only the love that is already built-in inside of you.

Karma gives you an opportunity to finally learn to love yourself. With the gift of multiple incarnations, you have the opportunity to learn to love yourself in spite of whether anyone else loves you or not. The need to have someone love you is because you simply do not love yourself enough. There is no denying that experiencing love through the use of the body is phenomenal, but there is also no denying that you have the potential to feel that same love without having sex. Your longing for sex is truly a longing for resolution. Resolution comes about over lifetimes. Because your soul believes that having sex with another person will connect you to your divine source, and that healing will take place upon that connection, you will long not only to have sex with this karmic partner, but also to stay connected to them. Your subconscious mind will feel such an overwhelming need to heal that it will convince your conscious mind that it has to stay even if the relationship is toxic.

Cheating and sex

First comes love, then marriage, then children, then cheating, then divorce. That has become the progression of relationships these days. How could something so beautiful turn into something so ugly? What is the real cause behind cheating on your partner? There are actually a couple of reasons behind this systematic pattern of cheating. The first one is ego.

When you're living in a monogamous relationship and someone comes along and flirts with you, it feels good to your ego. It peaks your low self-esteem. The ego needs to feel satisfied and it's so powerful that it can make you ignore your common sense. It will make you act compulsively. Once the passionate encounter is over, your soul may be left feeling empty. The reason it feels empty is because what your soul really wants is to be with a partner that fills all of your emotional, physical and mental needs.

I've had many a client who was about to jump off the deep end of monogamy by having an affair. Instead of asking if they should do it, they ask me whether or not the other person is really interested in them. Instead of asking how will this hurt my loved ones, including my children, they want to know if the other person is really interested in them or are they playing a game. They have no interest in personal integrity. They have no interest in the devastation they could cause in their family life. This emotional disruption was clearly shown in the movie *Unfaithful,* with Diane Lane and Richard Gere. She was in a happy marriage with a wonderful husband, yet when a young, hot, single man came along and complimented her, she was willing to throw it all away for passion in the sack. When he seduced her into his bed, her whole life was shattered. Her husband ended up killing her young lover in a moment of temporary insanity. It is also like the movie *Fatal Attraction*: when Michael Douglas' character had a one-night stand it almost destroyed his family's life. Even though it is a temporary high to have an affair, it rarely ends well.

In my healing sessions I've found that people on the precipice of having an affair are usually going through an intense cellular memory experience: karma. A negative karmic relationship is stirring wounds in their soul. Sometimes those wounds are from their childhood, and sometimes they are from a past life. When wounds surface, weak individuals will give into their karmic desire and have an affair. They will give into their passion before they take the time to understand their passion. Most of the people that cheat on their partners are misinterpreting the meaning of sexual attraction.

In the past people were able to avoid the pitfalls of physical attraction because they took the time to *know* the person before they married them. Even though they felt a strong attraction to another person, they stopped to think about the repercussions of their actions. Nowadays, people give in to their physical needs and ignore their conscious judgment. They ignore what they know to be right or wrong, and go for the satisfaction of ego. Afterwards, when the passion fades, they have tremendous feelings of guilt and self-hatred. They have an affair, the relationship doesn't work out and they hate themselves (this especially applies to women) for getting naked with someone they barely knew. That hatred just scratches the surface. God forbid their current partner finds out. Hearts are broken not only by the deception, but also by the betrayal. Before you give in to your ego's desires, stop and think how it would feel if someone did it to you – then *stop*, let the karma pass and don't go through with it. You have a choice.

Childhood and sex

As I stated earlier, I was sexually abused as a child. My inner child was deeply wounded from that abuse, the same as anyone who is abused sexually. As an adult, I had no conscious memory of that exploitation so it made it difficult to heal. My self-destructive actions did not have a logical explanation. I drank, smoked, dated bad boys, and had no self-respect. I had no idea why I was so cruel to myself. All I knew was that I could not stop myself from self-destructing. It was as if there was two of me: one that was abusing myself while the other was watching me do it. The watcher saw the negative actions but had no power to stop them. I had no idea why I hated myself so much. I had a couple of one-night stands yet had no idea why I would do that; I didn't even like sex. All told, I have had seven sexual partners in my entire life and that included two ex-husbands and a ten-year relationship. Compared to young people in this day and age, my seven sexual partners were minimal. Young people nowadays have seven sexual partners by the time they are sixteen years old. I had one fourteen-year-old client who had already been with more than forty boys. Promiscuity is the result of abuse or abandonment. Your wounded spirit is looking for love.

As an adult, all I really wanted was love, but to my inner child sex equated love. I kept searching for someone to love me. I believed, because of my abuse, that if someone wanted to have sex with me that meant they loved me. That was not true. After years of observing the anguish of the inner child, I am painfully aware that sexual abuse is one of the main culprits in adult self-destruction. I've observed hundreds of young women who were suffering guilt over a promiscuous lifestyle, yet they could not stop themselves. Whenever they slept with a guy and he didn't call, they would mentally torture themselves over their actions.

I am not a therapist, but through observing my clients I discovered that children who are sexually abused usually experience the same type of problems. Some of these are anxiety, sleep disturbances, substance abuse, and negative and failed relationships. On top of this they usually manifest abusive relationships. Plus they stay in those relationships beyond when they consciously know they should leave. To counter their uncomfortable internal feelings they cause themselves to suffer. They feel as if they did something wrong. The shame they feel internally manifests itself in negative life patterns.

Without the help of therapy, it's extremely difficult to overcome sexual abuse. I wish to God that I had been encouraged to get therapy. My childhood sucked, but coupled with the sexual abuse I was really f'd up. I needed therapy, but my family *never* would have suggested it. They swept everything under the rug and told me to move on and be strong. I really, truly believed that something was wrong with me because something was wrong with me. I was told that nothing was wrong with my life, but I felt horrible inside. I felt they were wrong, but they were the adults, so what the Hell did I know? What that taught me was to just work things out on my own, and not to seek out help. So, by the time I grew into adulthood, I was emotionally numb. I didn't feel anything. I was taught that it wasn't allowed.

I have worked on the wounds of my soul for years through spiritual guidance, but without the help of my therapist/friend I would have never discovered that I had been sexually abused. It was buried so deep within my subconscious that I had no conscious memory of it at all. Those painful memories surfaced only a few years ago, after I had been working on my subconscious wounds for over twenty years. It started with feelings of disdain for all women. I hated them. I hated being one. I hated their weakness and I didn't know why. With therapy I discovered that my childhood wounds of abuse were surfacing. With one treatment I discovered it wasn't other women's weaknesses that I hated, but my own. My inner child felt that she should have been strong enough to fend off her abuser. The truth was, I hated myself.

During our session, all of those memories came flooding into my consciousness. I was shocked yet at the same time joyously relieved – finally. The truth really does set you free. Those hidden memories had caused me to hate myself, to have a period of alcohol abuse, to be a bad mother and manifest bad relationships. If I had gotten help earlier in life I might not have suffered with years of self-hatred. My family's beliefs that you hid problems instead of facing them made my life a living Hell. I am stating facts here, not being a victim. I have worked very hard on releasing all my anger and hate for my family. Today, I view that as an opportunity for self-love. Once I discovered why I perpetuated victimhood, I stopped being a victim. That awakening helped me to understand why I was the way I was, and for that I will be eternally grateful.

Sex is never the cure for feeling unloved. Instead it is an impediment to self-love. When a victim of sexual abuse gets involved in a relationship, and that relationship ends, it deepens the wounds of the original infraction. The only way to manifest true love into your life is to first get it from yourself. Once you love yourself enough to heal the wounds created by sexual abuse, then you will manifest a loving partner.

If you have experienced sexual abuse, please get help. Do not try to deal with the suffering on your own. Like me, you may have painful memories that are blocked from your consciousness because it's too painful to remember. If you are in any way self-destructing, you have painful wounds that need to be addressed. Don't ignore them. We all need help from time to time, so go find a good therapist. Ask people you trust if they know of someone you can work with. Put messages out into the Universe to ask for help – help will come.

Tools for healing sexual issues

Writing this chapter on sex helped me to understand more about my own sexual thoughts. I am unique because I do not have a need for sex. As I stated earlier, I have been celibate for almost ten years now, and I would be perfectly content to spend the rest of my days without sex. I fill the need for the physical sexual experience by experiencing God directly. Through self-love, I have filled the void in my soul so that I do not need another human being in order to experience God. I have worked on healing the human need for a connection to God through the use of a sexual experience. Writing this chapter also helped me to understand the confusion and chaotic sexual thoughts of the human race.

What helped me to get to this level of awareness was to stop having sex. Don't panic yet; you don't have to stop having sex to fix the wounds that are causing you to be f'd up. Even though abstaining from sex is the best way to heal old wounds, it's not the only way. Most of the time healing those unhealthy desires requires paying attention to your harmful thoughts and loving yourself out of them. However, if you are in the midst of a promiscuous marathon, I'd strongly suggest you stop having sex for a while.

If you find yourself having sex with someone you've just met, or if all you want to do is have sex, then you need to take a good, long look at your self-esteem. Your soul *needs* to have sex because you do not love yourself enough. You are desperately trying to get someone, anyone to love you. Sex makes you feel loved. In order to heal yourself from the confusion surrounding sex, there are some proactive things you need to do:

1. Love yourself

Simple – not easy. All you need to do is to say to yourself four- to five-hundred times a day, "I love me." You don't even have to make extra time during the day to do this – just do it during your normal everyday activities like showering, driving alone in your car, going to the bathroom, cooking, or whatever. While you go about your day, just take advantage of those moments when you are alone to love yourself. Since we've already established that your subconscious mind needs repetition, you need to say "I love me" at least four- to five-hundred times in order for it to resonate. Instead of allowing your mind to think whatever it wants to during these opportune times, tell it to think that you love yourself instead.

2. Get therapy

If you are consciously aware of the fact that you've been sexually abused, find a good, recommended therapist and get help. There is nothing to be ashamed of and you need to get to the source of your issues.

3. Become consciously aware of your sexual needs.

If you ever feel yourself wanting to have sex with what could only be considered a stranger, don't do it. Instead walk away and spend time telling yourself how much you love yourself. If you feel a need to watch porn, it's indicative of your soul's need to reconnect with God. Instead of watching something that desecrates the truth behind a sexual experience, spend time instead reconnecting with your soul by connecting with your heart. Put your hand on your heart, and imagine that your soul is in there. Connect with it. Talk to it. Smile, and recognize the God within you. If this does not open your heart, then try masturbation. But instead of just feeling the physical aspect of an orgasm, focus on the emotional aspects of your soul. After the orgasm notice how you feel; notice if you have any unresolved emotions surfacing. Let yourself cry if that's what you feel. Let yourself laugh if it felt good to have that physical release. I am not saying to masturbate until you create a need in your soul for masturbation; I'm saying to create a release for your emotions when you have a need for sex.

Sexual truth

I believe the reason the world is becoming more obsessed with sex and sexuality is an internal fear that we will lose sight of our God-like nature. Sex helps us to remember God, so with the increase in trauma and drama in your world, your soul is looking for a way to escape back to your truth. The more chaotic your physical world becomes the more you will long for sexual encounters, because you are terrified you will forget God.

An unhealthy need for sex, or having perverted thoughts of deviant sexual behavior, means that your soul is suffering. It means there is something terribly wrong and out of balance. Having those needs means that you have painful wounds in your soul. If you take the time to pay attention to those unhealthy desires, you will be able to get to the source of that pain. Looking at and then understanding the pain of your soul gives you a tremendous opportunity for soul growth.

5
LOVE

"Love is composed of a single soul inhabiting two bodies."

—Aristotle

After I had finished writing this book, I had the realization that I had left out one of the most important reasons your life can be f'd up: LOVE. This may be the fifth chapter in the book, but it was the last one written.

Love is the most significant ingredient of your life. Love is also the most misinterpreted of all those ingredients. We innately want to love so that we can overcome our separateness. Our souls are all one, so when we encounter physical love it connects us with that oneness. When you have love in your life, the rest of your life is better. Love is divine; it is constant, but the world does not exhibit that. Our world is ruled by fear, which initiates rules for love. In reality, love is a pure existence within itself; it is a glorious feeling, but in your illusionary world it has stipulations. Love isn't easy; but it's effortless. Your soul is set on automatic pilot to love. Love is divinely intended to break open the seal of past heartache. You cannot heal your damaged spirit if you do not love.

Instead of love, society teaches you that your life priority should be career and material possessions. Societal judgment declares that the money you carry in your wallet is more important than the love you carry in your heart. If you ever hope to know love, you have to take the risk of hurting. Great love and great achievement requires great risk.

Although I haven't been in a relationship for over ten years, I still feel love in my heart every day. Love is a beautiful, ecstatic, joyous, all-encompassing feeling that is often indescribable, but most importantly it is self-contained. Love comes standard on all forms of humans. When I sat down to write this chapter my daughter said to me that in order to be considered an "expert" on love I needed to be in a loving relationship. I begged to differ. My expertise lies with love itself. I experience love internally. I don't need anything or anyone outside myself in order to feel it. I love sharing my life with others, but I don't *need* them in order to feel good about myself. I don't ever feel lonely or alone. I'm not saying having a partner is a bad thing, just that needing one is. Buddhists call it the art of detachment. When a seeker confronted a Buddhist master about the attachment they thought he had to his grandchildren, he said they are like a dip in the river; he enjoys the river but doesn't take it home with him when he leaves.

Love = pain

Why is it that the love for another appears to be painful? How can love start out feeling so good and end up feeling so bad? One reason is because you have unrealistic expectations of it. You assign rules to love. Love has nothing to do with a long-lasting relationship; it's a separate entity entirely. Love is just love. The stipulations and expectations that you put on love are what hurt – not the love itself.

First you fall in love, then announce to the world the perfection of your new lover, and then spend the next several years trying to change them. You demand that they fold the towels a certain way, wear their clothes or hair the way you like it, take out the trash, or dictate how they spend their time. Household duties take precedence over love. In order to live happily ever after, the so-called love of your life had better play by your rules. What does any of that have to do with love? Absolutely nothing. When you force a partner to acquiesce to your desires then you are not being accepting, just manipulative.

One of the greatest misconceptions of love is that you can fall out of it. Love never dies or goes away. The illusion dies, not the love. You don't ever fall out of love with someone else, because the loss you feel has nothing to do with the other party, but everything to do with you. The heartbreak you feel when the relationship ends is because you were misinterpreting your feelings in the first place.

Most of the time, you fall in love with who you *hope* your partner will be. You want to believe they are perfect, so you believe they are perfect. The first thing you should do when you meet a potential partner is to find everything wrong with them that you can. They're going to show you the good traits, but you have to live with the bad ones. When you see their shortcomings first there is no illusion, just acceptance and love.

Fear of love

Love should never be feared; it should be felt. Men and

women alike are terrified of their hearts. Society has put a psychological twist on love with mental concepts attached to feelings. Although love can drive you crazy you should not confuse the feeling of love with the reason for hurting. When the relationship ends, it's not the loss of love that feels bad; it's the judgment that causes you to be in pain. Without expectations or mental evaluation, the feeling of love is pretty damn good.

When you feel pain in a relationship, it's not because love hurts, it's because love is the catalyst to release childhood dramas. Without healing, life is like the movie *Groundhog Day*, different day – same wounds. Childhood traumas are cyclical; you will continue to manifest the same ones until you heal them. Love was divinely designed as a tool to process the lack of self-love you have stored in your soul. Love is the UP button on the elevator of life. You can't go up unless you push the button.

Over the years I have heard so many people say that they are desperate for love but are afraid to date; they are afraid of getting hurt. I tell them that not dating defeats the purpose because they are already hurting. What do you have to lose by seeking love? Can the loss of a partner be worse than being unhappy and feeling alone?

You were created for the purpose of experiencing both good and bad. Love will *never* prevent you from experiencing pain. Love is the trigger to release internal anguish. Love is always the catalyst.

Over the past eleven years of being single I've grown in leaps and bounds spiritually. When my ten-year relationship ended, the last thing I wanted was a man in my life. In that relationship I was needy, subservient, and fearful – not exactly the characteristics of a good partner. I intuitively knew that if I ever hoped to have a love alliance, I needed to work on me first. If I expected a good partner to come along, I first had to become one. I'm still not dating, but it's not because

I'm afraid of being hurt or suffering from a broken heart. I don't date because I'm complete. If I met someone that I felt a positive, loving connection with I would absolutely pursue it. I realize the spiritual growth opportunity that having a partner gives the soul. I know self-love feels good, but with a partner it's divine. I know I want to give my partner the greatest gift of life: to live his own truth, not mine. I want a partner who has conversations, not confrontations. I want my soul to express love at its maximum potential, so I know there could still be miniscule particles of childhood drama buried inside, but thanks to my knowledge of love I welcome that pain. Unless and until I meet someone that has the same spiritual understanding of life as I do, I will joyously remain detached. The best compliment I ever had was when my daughter told a friend of hers, when they asked her if I were dating, "I can't even imagine the kind of man it would take to get my mother's attention."

The misperceptions of love

"Don't let someone become your everything, because when they're gone you have nothing!"

Kenya Mitchell

From my years of empathic intuitive experience, I've noticed three misperceptions of love. Having these false expectations can make you sad, angry, disappointed and heartbroken.

1. You feel love because someone else gives it to you.

You never need another person or thing in order

to feel love. Just because you do not have a partner, wife, or husband does not mean you cannot feel love. Love is internal, not external. It's an illusion that anyone ever *gives* it to you. The reason you believe that someone gives you love is because of how you feel about yourself when they choose you. Your self-esteem is heightened because you believe you are loved. When you don't love yourself enough you rely solely on their love. Being dependent on someone else for love makes you needy. Needy is ugly. If you give someone the power to make you feel better about yourself, you are also giving him or her the power to make you feel worse.

In order to feel love, all you need to do is open your heart and feel it. There is only one kind of love. Whether you feel love for your children, your lover, your husband, your pets, your friends, or your co-workers, it is all the same love. There is only one kind of love; the only difference is in how you express it.

2. If you haven't had or aren't in a long-term relationship it's because you are unlovable.

I have to say that this is more of a female than male trait. Women make the assumption that they are ugly, fat, or stupid if they aren't in a relationship. Did you ever stop to think that maybe there is a divine purpose in being alone? Maybe you have this time to yourself because your soul needs a *time out*. There are a plethora of reasons the soul needs a breather, but all of them are beneficial.

The truth is that *not* being in a relationship can be one of the most beneficial times of your life. Being alone can be one of the most loving things you can do for yourself. Not being with somebody else gives you much needed self-discovery time.

If you take advantage of it, time alone can bring about a greater understanding of your wounds. When you do that, you don't take those wounds into the next relationship with you. Taking the time out to heal a broken heart will prevent a pattern of pain. When you do not heal the pain, you recreate it.

When you are in-between relationships you need to regroup the emotional troops. You need to look at your past relationships to discover what you learned about yourself from them. Take the time to observe, not judge, your behavior. Look at your trigger points. Think about what your past lovers did that upset you, and then look back at your childhood to see where that emotion began. The wounds of the child *are* the wounds of the adult.

Each and every lover can trigger a different agony. There are layers upon layers of your soul. Remember the soul knows no space and time; as far as it's concerned it's all going on at the same time. Your new lover was your old lover in another lifetime. You carry those unresolved emotions with you into this lifetime. When you meet up again, the old emotions resurface giving you another opportunity to heal. Even if you negate the possibility of past lives from the equation you will still have your childhood pain surface. Just when you think you've healed all the old wounds, you meet someone new and BOOM! up comes the anguish.

It's not easy, but with mutual respect, communication, understanding and compassion you can love your way through a bad relationship and move on. You can never truly feel the love inside until you release all the past suffering. Whenever a negative karmic relationship comes into your life you should be grateful for its gift of the liberation of anguish.

3. If a relationship ends it's because you did something wrong.

Successful relationships are never based on longevity. Sometimes, tremendous spiritual growth can come from a one-night stand. The growth comes from the lessons learned, not the amount of time you spend together. Sometimes, being able to walk away is more valuable than staying. Society tells you that if you love someone you are supposed to live happily ever after together. Some relationships are not created to last forever, but are for the purpose of fixing a negative karmic experience instead. Love is forever; love is eternal; but partners are karmic.

When a relationship ends and you are in pain, the pain is not caused from the loss of love from the other person; it's caused from *a lack of love for yourself.*

I wanted that sentence to stand-alone because it is so important in understanding love. You hurt because you don't love you. It hurts because you take it personally. You hurt because your soul doesn't feel it is worthy of love when someone you've loved leaves. You hurt because you believed that the reason you felt love in the first place was because someone was giving you that love. When they went away you no longer loved yourself.

Negative love

Love is *never* the reason to stay in a negative relationship.

Negative love is a love that you know you should leave, but you just can't. From a cerebral standpoint you get why it won't work, but you stay because of your emotions. It hurts you to be with this person, but you're convinced that love requires you to stay. Staying has nothing to do with love, but instead a lack of self-love. Negative love is about self-esteem.

If someone is cruel and unloving to you, you should leave no matter how much love you ostensibly feel for him or her. You don't leave because you're afraid that no one else will love you. If you valued yourself enough, it wouldn't matter.

Don't put all your eggs in one love basket; there will always be someone else to love. Our loving God created a world of endless – not limited – amounts of love.

Healing a broken heart

A broken heart is not gender- or age qualified. Every human being, at sometime in their life, experiences a broken heart.

A broken heart is never because love is gone, it's because you are judging yourself.

An important tool to heal your broken spirit is to take conscious control of it – get in the game. Self-love heals all wounds.

There are three steps to healing a broken heart:

1. Find the gift

Each and every person you love has a gift for you. If you're paying attention you can see it. Your lover's negative attributes are usually mirror images of your own. When you can see the parts of you that are negative by looking at them, it's a gift. As soon as you find the gift, you heal.

2. Self-love fest

One of the quickest ways to lift out of heartache is to love *you* more. After a break-up, say to yourself, "I love me" four- to five-hundred times a day. On a piece of paper write down what you like about you. Spend time loving everything about yourself instead of judging everything about yourself.

3. Find the source

Another element in healing is to dig deep into your soul and find the source of your heartache. Judgment of self is usually the cause of a broken heart and that starts in childhood. Look at your past partners and find a similarity between their negative characteristics and those of your parents. It may take some time, but when you have a realization of the root source of your broken heart, your heart will mend.

When you allow yourself to be fearless with love, you have the opportunity for tremendous spiritual growth, to forever be *IN LOVE*.

6
PAIN IS AN OPPORTUNITY

Can you name one person that doesn't suffer in some way? Do you know anyone that lives a life free of pain? No, I'm sure you don't. If people are not suffering physical pain then they are experiencing some kind of emotional or mental pain. It doesn't matter if the pain is physical, mental, or emotional; the pain begins within. When you heal the wounds or negative beliefs of the soul, you heal the conditions of your physical life.

It is part of human nature to feel discomfort. It doesn't seem fair, but pain is a way of life. Your spirit always has more to learn and pain is the motivator. You suffer in order to understand. You incarnate to this plane of existence for the learning possibilities; you come to remember how great you really are at your core by being the opposite of your core. You cannot possibly learn about yourself unless you feel something other than pleasure. Pleasure doesn't perpetuate the growth of your soul; only pain reveals the truth about your internal belief system. Pain brings about a tremendous opportunity for spiritual growth.

I mentioned in the chapter on God that God has a different perspective than you about pain. But that is not the only reason God does not step in to save you. God doesn't step in to save you because God knows he/she doesn't have to. God created you in his image, which means you have the power of God within you. God doesn't need to step in, because God already is in. God is inside of you. The same divine spark that created everything you see is within you. If you really want to heal, you will heal. I am not saying that all a person has to do to heal cancer is to be consciously aware of the emotional reason behind the disease. The soul is complicated, yet so simple. There are layers upon layers of wounds to be addressed before you can ever get to the root source of the disease. It's only after you get to the root of the disease that you have the ability to heal. You must uncover the truth behind your illness. Getting to the root source of the illness is all encompassing; it takes dedication to get to a level of understanding of the reason behind your energy being stagnated. Stagnated energy creates disease. Illness is caused by a lack of attention. You know when your soul is in pain, yet you continue to ignore it. You ignore it long enough for disease to manifest in your body. When your emotional life is in turmoil, you get physically sick until you resolve your emotions. The disease makes you pay attention to your spirit. Your body was divinely designed to reveal the physical signs of your emotional damage.

There will never come a time that you do not, in some shape or form, experience pain. Pain is an opportunity to discover the unresolved emotions of your soul. There is always more to learn. As you heal your wounds, you will experience fewer and fewer difficulties, as well as shorter suffering times, but there will always be something to heal.

The benefits of overcoming adversity are divine; it is a good thing.

If you can learn to embrace painful experiences you can change your level of happiness. Feelings of anger, disappointment, jealousy, hatred, and sadness are all good things if you can understand the need your soul has to feel them. Anytime you have a fearful feeling you have the opportunity to tap into something within you that needs help. Those ostensibly negative feelings are actually good for you if you pay attention to them. When you have those negative, hurtful feelings it's as if God or the Universe is trying to help you to understand yourself better. Humans are always looking for external signs from God to help them know what to do in life, yet they never look at their emotions as those signs from God. Your souls are designed to heal; healing is what you do best. You innately want to heal because it feels so damn good when you do. You do not need external signs to tell you what to do or where to go in life, you have an amazing internal radar system that shows you how to navigate your life: your body. Your body is trying to show you the pain of your soul when your stomach knots up, you get a headache, your chest tightens – or worst-case scenario – you get sick or diseased.

Your friends, families, careers, and events of your life are designed to trigger unresolved emotions. Everything that happens in your life happens so you can heal those unresolved emotions. All negative emotions and experiences are really positive with the proper perspective. Stop thinking that feeling bad is a bad thing and start thinking of it as a yummy treat from God to help end the suffering of your soul. You were designed with such precision that you never have to wonder about your emotional issues – they show up all by themselves. You have this unrealistic conviction that feeling bad is a sign that something is wrong with you, when in actuality it's showing you that something is right.

Whenever you are ready for growth, the bad feelings inside of you surface. You may consciously walk around in denial of your feelings, but your soul is never in denial. You can never avoid growth, you can ignore it for a while but you can't avoid it. Whether you deny your truth or not, the pain will surface. When you stop running from pain and instead start looking at it objectively, you will heal.

Because families trigger your pain better than acquaintances and co-workers, the most tremendous emotional growth comes from families. My only family is my daughter. I disassociated myself from my blood relatives many years ago. I did this is because I needed to seek my truth, and I knew I couldn't do that while being around my family. There were too many agonizing memories to overcome; I needed clarity. I needed to discover my truth instead of theirs.

My daughter and I have a wonderful relationship now. We are bound together in ways most mothers and daughters only dream about. We realize we have a very good relationship. That being said, we still fight. We fight because we each want the other to live life the way we live our own. Being human, we fight for some semblance of control. Our most recent fight was, like most of them, over something insignificant in the greater scheme of things. I don't like anyone, including myself, to be ridiculed. It doesn't hurt my feelings when people do it, I just don't see the point to it. I don't follow the current society's ideas of funny, which is insulting your friends and family. My daughter believes otherwise. It's funny to her to point out other people's idiosyncrasies. I know that the way I live my life is not her cup of tea, just as her way isn't mine. In the past, when I told her that I don't think her pointing out my obvious idiosyncratic ways is appropriate, she thought I was being too sensitive. My feelings are that I'm not being sensitive; I just want her to accept my uniqueness. We both know how

I am; my idiosyncrasies are very irritating to her, but I don't need a constant reminder of my weird habits. There is no right or wrong – just a difference of opinion.

Unfortunately, this particular fight got really ugly. I was very disappointed in myself when I left her because during the fight she provoked anger in me. I was disappointed because I reacted in a negative way instead of acting in my truth. We all have opportunities to react with an old pattern or create a new one. I failed miserably at creation. I immediately went home to awaken to the reason I reacted so adversely to her. I believe I discovered the source of my reaction of anger, which was previous life persecutions, but I am still looking for more cellular memories.

I tell you this because I know that I am on the path to discovering everything I can about myself. I want to know everything about my internal world. I work very hard on myself, and I believe that I have a greater understanding of the illusion of this planet than most. Yet, when I was faced with an opportunity to show that I am more aware, I let my buttons get pushed and I reacted. You know the old saying: if someone is always pushing your buttons, stop having any buttons to push. More often than not there is a gap between what you know to be truth, and actually living the truth. I did not live my truth that day. Ugh. The moral to this story is that no matter how much you work on yourself, you will still have more to work on. It also showed me how far I have to go to living my truth. It's easy for me to be connected to my knowledge when it is with someone other than my daughter. I rarely get my buttons pushed in other relationships. She is obviously my greatest source for growth. Thanks to that ostensibly negative fight, I realized my reactions, changed them, and now we don't fight much anymore and when we do it's short lived. We fight because we are human. Our minds have an agenda, and that agenda is ego. Each of our egos wanted the other one to be wrong because we have a *need* to be right. But I digress. That fight caused us pain, but the pain wasn't from that particular scenario, but instead from each of our own old internal wounds. The fight made it obvious that we both had some unresolved emotions between us. We both worked on ourselves and the pain went away.

Ignoring the pain

When you choose to ignore your pain, you open the door to disease or addictions. You think that something is wrong with you so you try to cover up the pain. You find a way to escape to the materialistic world in order to stop the pain. You do everything in your power to hide from it. You might throw temper tantrums, scream at loved ones, slap someone in the face, or even perpetrate a crime in an attempt to *not* accept what's going on internally. Shopaholics cover their pain by buying material possessions; alcoholics try to drink it away; socialites surround themselves with people so they don't have to be alone; child molesters and rapists repeat the pattern of abuse. No matter what you feel, you don't want others to know your true feelings, so you hide them. You're afraid others will judge you, but the reason you do that is because *you* are judging you.

Your soul will continue its self-destructive behavior until you hit rock bottom. Hitting rock bottom is a good thing. When a person is at the end of their rope it's the perfect time to let go of the rope and grow. There are only two choices you have when it comes to pain and fear: face it or deny it. Facing it means you heal and have an opportunity for happiness; denying it makes you continue to suffer.

Your soul is always in the game of growth whether you consciously accept it or not. So you might as well embrace the opportunity, stop judging yourself and get in the game.

Ignorance of the game does not mean you aren't playing it. So *get in the game!*

Wounds

As individuals, our personal life scenarios are always different, but as a whole the emotional opportunity is always the same. Remember the reason for your existence is for emotional knowledge. Your wounds may surface because you get fired from your job, your husband cheats on you, your child is doing drugs, a loved one has just been diagnosed with cancer, your best friend lied to you, or your own body is sick. Your neighbor's wounds may surface because their house is in foreclosure, they are going through a divorce, or a parent has just died. Whatever life scenario you are experiencing, you are experiencing it so that your soul can grow and get back to its origin of love. Pain always reveals something amiss within.

Embrace and accept

Once you change your perspective about your painful existence, you can change your life. Take a couple of moments right now and think about the struggles in your life; think about the past obstacles that you have faced. Now think about how great you felt about yourself after you overcame those obstacles. Once you understood and grew from the adversities, your perspective changed. You became more God-like. When you think about how much knowledge you gained from the supposed failures in your life, you will realize the importance of emotional knowledge.

How does one go about embracing their pain? To understand your pain you must first acknowledge it. By acknowledge I do not mean judge; I mean to look at it objectively. Look at it as an observer. Where is the emotional pain really coming from? Is it coming from the current moment or is it possibly coming from your childhood? When you don't heal a fear you continue to experience the fear. Unresolved emotions will continue to cause you anxiety until you heal them. So the pain you feel in your relationships today may be caused from a painful relationship with your father as a child. Your parents are the original source of your pain in this lifetime. Whether it's from abandonment or physical and emotional abuse, your parents give you your first opportunity to experience emotional pain.

The soul cannot stand pain; pain is a lack of love. Your soul consists entirely of love, so when there is an aspect of self that is in pain, the soul has an innate need to heal. When the soul is ready to heal, it will manifest circumstances that cause you to pay attention. Those hurtful circumstances will reveal your wounds. If you ignore your emotional and mental pains long enough, they manifest into physical disease. Physical *dis*-ease is a sign that your soul is sick. Whenever the body gets sick, the soul is talking.

Life purpose and pain

Your purpose in life is to resolve unresolved emotions. Almost every one of my clients at one time or another will ask me about their purpose regarding their career. Your career path is chosen because of the opportunity to experience the emotions that the career path will give you. Your chosen career gives you an opportunity to create the emotional situation your soul needs. The soul's purpose in incarnating is not for money, fame, career, big houses, and cars; you come here to grow emotionally, and in the process learn to love yourself. You do not incarnate to go to Harvard and be able to impress others with the intellect; unless of course that path will help you to grow emotionally. If your self-esteem needs to evolve by being college educated, then you'll have a desire to go to college. All of those thoughts are part of the illusion of life. You choose the career, the educational level you achieve, poverty, great wealth, fame or a complete lack of recognition for the _soul_ purpose of growing emotionally. For some souls, being wealthy gives them the most advantage for emotional growth, yet for others being poor will be most advantageous. Or if, for example, you choose to be an actor, you are possibly trying to work on the feelings caused by rejection; actors get rejected ninety percent of the time. Celebrities' lives are also an open book professionally as well as personally. If they do a bad job in a movie, everyone sees and talks about it. If their marriage falls apart, they are on the cover of every magazine in the world. That creates great opportunity for self-awareness. An actor is forced to learn to love him or herself no matter what anyone else thinks. I believe this gives them an amazing opportunity for growth. Everyone on this planet chooses opportunities to grow emotionally, so why would celebrities be any different?

The pain of death

Death happens to all of us, but if God created the magnificence of us, then it should be a piece of cake for this divine being to heal disease. The human body is a wonderment and God created that, so why can't God miraculously heal a dying person? Many people believe that God punishes us for our transgressions. My family had the convoluted idea that when someone died, it was because God was pulling the strings and caused their death. My family believed that if someone died it was because God needed them more than we did. They told me that crazy belief when my mother died. I didn't believe it then and I don't believe it now. Death, like every other emotional event is an opportunity to grow from the devastation of that emotional event. As much as you would like to believe that there is a divine puppet master, it just doesn't make sense. If God isn't taking our loved ones to use in heaven, then what could possibly be the reason for death? Death, like everything else that happens in our physical Universe, is for the purpose of spiritual growth. The pain that you endure from the death of a loved one gives your soul an opportunity to release old wounds.

God is not in charge of when you die; you are. God does not need you to help him/her in heaven. You are self-contained. You make all the choices of pain and the opportunity it provides. Your conscious, sub-conscious and higher consciousness makes the decision to incorporate pain into your life. You choose life, but you also choose death. With the exception of suicide the conscious mind does not usually choose to die. Death is decided from a sub-conscious and higher conscious perspective. Before you incarnate you give yourself different times and circumstances that will end your life. Your higher consciousness knows exactly what it is doing when it chooses death. With your limited consciousness of how things work in the Universe, you can't possible comprehend why someone would choose to die. But you must realize that to the higher consciousness of the loved one that has passed, it makes sense. Sometimes death comes about because the fears of the sub-conscious mind were not faced, and the body got sick. If you are ill, in physical pain, you must pay attention to the emotional dis-ease behind the illness, heal those thoughts, and then take the action needed to heal. For most people, it's only when you leave your body in death that you can understand the true reason of your death.

How can you take advantage of the painful opportunities God gives you for growth? Recognition, acknowledgement, and perspective. *Recognize* that the pain is trying to tell you something, *acknowledge* what that something is and change your *perspective* about the pain. Instead of suffering, rejoice that you are cleansing your soul of negative thoughts and then celebrate the healing that will change your perspective. Instead of seeing the pain through your own eyes, you will see it through the joyous eyes of the creator. Seize the opportunity to change your life by understanding your anguish.

Tools for healing pain

As I've stated before, in order to stop the pattern of pain you must first acknowledge it. You must get in the game. Whenever you are in pain, you must seize the opportunity to recognize the truth and change your perspective. Three ways to take advantage of the opportunity pain gives you are:

1. Journal
Writing down the thoughts you have will help you to understand those thoughts. Human beings are great thinkers – they think all the time. In fact, they never stop thinking. They are set on automatic pilot to think. In order to heal, you must first realize what it is you're thinking. Taking a few moments everyday to write down some of your negative thoughts is mandatory if you want to heal. You can't heal a thought if you don't realize you're having it. Take the time to recognize when you are feeling badly about yourself. You feel badly because you are thinking badly. Go buy a tiny notebook to write down some of those thoughts. Use the mantra, "Well look at that, I just thought I was stupid." Then write down what made you think you were stupid. When you're writing your thoughts in your journal, you are not necessarily trying to figure out the source of

the negative thought. The journal's purpose is to *get you in the game.* It will help you to habitually notice your negative thoughts. After you have practiced writing down negative thoughts enough that it becomes habitual, you can try to figure out the source of those negative thoughts.

2. Meditate

Over the past several years, I've met a lot of people who say they can't or don't want to meditate. I think this is because they are confused about what meditation is really about. Most people meditate in some form or another. Some dance, some sing, some read, some write, or some meditate through art. For the purpose of healing your pain, you should meditate for silence of thought. All I'm talking about is NOT thinking. Start by spending five minutes a day just closing your eyes and focusing on one particular thing. Stare at a pencil or candle for five minutes and only think about that pencil or candle and dismiss any other thoughts that you have. Recognize that you're *thinking* and stop it. Once you've mastered the fine art of thinking only one thought at a time, you can practice thinking about nothing. Meditation is designed to calm your mind. By focusing on your breath instead of on your thoughts you calm the mind. Meditation should not be complicated; your mind already has "complicated" mastered. Some hints to a clearing meditation:

    a. Sit comfortably in a quiet space (light candles if you want).

    b. Start focusing on your breath.

    c. Notice your lungs as you breath in and out.

    d. If you're having difficulty focusing on your

breath, then focus on the candle. See every aspect of the candle: the flame, the color, and the shape. Only think about the candle.

e. Gently let go of any thoughts that enters your mind. Say "Bye-bye thought, catch ya later!" Then refocus on your breathing.

3. Celebrate

Accepting that you're only human and that human beings are divinely designed to be messed up should bring you some peace. When you stop yourself from judging yourself for being human and celebrate your growth, you release old karmic patterns. Those karmic patterns are what keep you stuck in the wheel of shame. Whenever you *notice* judgment of yourself and you stop that judgment, celebrate. Give yourself a cheer. "Yay me!" Toast yourself with either a glass of wine or juice. "Whoopee, I did it. I changed my thoughts. I healed my soul!" Celebrate the fact that you just had another opportunity to discover yourself and you took advantage of that opportunity. *Celebrate you!*

7
INNER CHILD

One of the major causes of someone's life being f'd up stems from the damage done to them as a child. That damage caused pain, that pain is stored in your cells as your inner child. Your inner child is the purest version of you, the one closest to your truth, the part of you that embraced optimism and joy and knew exactly who he or she wanted to be. Your inner child is also that part of you that has not healed the painful memories and emotions of your childhood. Those unresolved emotions create a *need* in your soul to heal. That soul need will continue to manifest similar painful scenarios in your life until you resolve the pain from your childhood. Basically, external boo-boos happen because we have internal boo-boos. In order to heal these boo-boos, we have to go back to the source of the pain. There is a moment in time that the pain was created. In that moment the soul stored the pain in your cells. Since that moment you have been piling on the pain. To heal you need to go back through the layers of suffering to get to the source of your boo-boo in this lifetime.

Before your soul incarnates, you purposely choose parents that will trigger the wounds you wish to heal. You enter your body with the intention to heal those things that you do not love about yourself. On the other side, between lives, and with the help of other beings, you take stock of your growth and spiritual development. You look for holes in your soul and look at yourself with a greater degree of understanding than you ever could *in the body* because you're self-realized. On the other side, you meet with a spiritual council who, without judgment, help you decide the emotional purpose of each incarnation. They help you determine which aspects of yourself are yet unresolved. This is why you don't come into the body pure as fresh Arctic snow; rather you come into the body imperfect, with a desire and perspective about the wounds you *want* to come into the body to heal. Part of the healing process begins with birth and your parents.

Your parents are usually polar opposites of what you innately know your truth to be and are therefore chosen so you can quickly learn who you are by seeing who you're not. Once you enter your body, your parents and other elders immediately, systematically, and unconsciously inflict pain upon you, which makes you question your own beliefs. They teach you what they believe to be right and wrong. They teach you as their parents taught them. Their stories become your stories. Their fears become your fears. Their lies become your lies. When they want your opinions, they give them to you. Someday, after you realize what your own stories, beliefs, fears, lies and opinions are, you'll be able to rejoice in your own wisdom.

When I was a child my father told me that in order for Jesus to love me I had to be a good girl; that in order for me to go to heaven I had to be a good girl. I thought I was a good girl. I was sweet, loving, kind, and happy; but after enough time under my father's influence and enough times of being told I actually wasn't a good girl, I started to believe him. I became confused about the definitions of good and bad. Because you're taught from the beginning of your life that parents and adults know what's best for you, I, like everyone else, mindlessly obeyed, even though I internally disagreed.

You're designed to disagree not only to drive your parents crazy, but also to help you understand yourself and learn to value your own opinion. I remember that as a child I always wanted to be outside during sun, rain, snow, sleet, or hail. I didn't care – I just wanted to be outside. One day, when I started to head outside, my grandmother stopped me and told me to put on my coat, because I was cold. I told her I wasn't cold, but she insisted I was. I was pretty sure I wasn't, but she was the adult, so I assumed I was wrong, so my coat went on. My rational mind tried to understand this theory of wearing a coat when I wasn't cold and in that moment, as seemingly insignificant as it was, I learned not to trust my own opinion. Each additional so-called insignificant incident creates a pattern of belief. Whether intentionally or inadvertently, your parents teach you to *not* trust your own feelings.

A classic example of a parent making me question my truth was my father's famous saying, as he was about to spank me, "This hurts me more than it hurts you." I was absolutely certain that his hand or belt (depending on his mood that day) hurt my tiny butt more than his giant hand. Again, I was very confused. Small incidents like this cause a deep mistrust of your own feelings, so you systematically shut them off over time. This is the reason bad habits are passed down from generation to generation until someone comes along to break the pattern. Enter the rebel. Rebellious children are just trying to find their true selves. They are acutely aware that something isn't right and refuse to believe what they're told. Somewhere deep inside they remember their truth and are trying to actualize it.

Unfortunately, the rebel will often get tired of fighting and join the crowd mentality. In my case, I got so tired of fighting with my father that it became easier to just give in. Instead of getting yet another beating, I simply, robotically did what he told me to do. I gave in and took on his belief system. He wore my strong constitution down to nothing, and weakened my spirit. I started believing that I was stupid. I believed that I did not have a chance in Hell of being successful. I believed that my sisters were amazing and I was a piece of crap. He won, I lost. He finally, systematically, crippled my spirit. This is what happens to children when they take on their family's beliefs; they just get tired of struggling against the tyranny. They lose their identity and take on their parents' way of life. Essentially, without realizing it, they become their parents.

Inadvertent hurt

The bulk of the healing work I do is helping clients remove childhood wounds. Whether you were locked in a closet as a child or told you were stupid for drawing on the walls in your bedroom, you stored those painful memories in your cells. Children know that it hurts when you insult them, but they have no power to stop you from hurting them. Adults forget about the powerful weapon they have over children: words. As adults, you have to be acutely aware of how *you* behave in front of your children. You have to stop and think before you utter words of defamation directed towards them. They hold these memories, thoughts, and words in their cells for life, just like you did. As adults you should remember the pain your parents inflicted on you and break the pattern with your own children. Don't pass down the agony.

During a regression session, a woman in her thirties recalled witnessing her younger brother and their mother in a sexual encounter. She remembered her brother crying out for help and not being able to help him. She remembered trying to burst into the room, but having the door slammed in her face. She is now an emotionally distraught woman. She has never felt worthy of happiness because she subconsciously blamed herself for her brother's pain. Who wouldn't? Can you imagine the pain after witnessing that atrocity and being powerless to stop it? After our healing session, she contracted a urinary tract infection. She was physically releasing the anger she had stored for over twenty-five years. The urinary tract infection symbolized anger; she was literally pissed off at her mother for inflicting that pain on her and her brother. Even though, as a child, she was truly powerless to help, she still blamed herself. Releasing a memory like that can bring about amazing changes in one's emotional health. Releasing that anger gave her a chance to finally heal.

Not everyone experiences that level of deep, intense pain, but you each have your own variations and levels that need to be addressed and healed. Think back. Is there something buried in your past that's holding you back now? Is there something from your childhood for which you blame yourself? Is it keeping you from living your most joyful life?

Leaving the light

Your soul comes into the body set on automatic pilot to blame itself for any suffering you experience. Your soul is emotionally more astute, considering you have just re-entered the physical realm, so you're super sensitive to the darkness of negativity or the lack of love. As babies, you only know the light side of the soul and are very susceptible to anything less than light, as light is love. When a child sees darkness, they know something is energetically wrong, but instead of blaming the adults, they blame themselves. As an adult, you have anesthetized yourself to negative energy, but with children the negativity resonates to the core of their soul. If, for example, you observe your parents fighting, you automatically assume that you did something wrong and caused the fight. You blame yourself and in doing so, you fail to love yourself and the wounds are created.

You carry those childhood wounds with you into your adult life and that is what causes you to be emotionally and mentally unstable. You react to situations in your life with these unresolved emotions. You react because your childhood wounds have beaten you down and you want to fight back. Imagine how you would feel if you woke up every day to someone slapping you in the face. After only a few days of being slapped, you would become very irritated, defensive and edgy. From then on, whenever anyone insulted you, you would want to slap him or her. That's what happens to children. They get hurt, then that emotional pain builds up inside of them over time; eventually it makes them want to lash out. Their anger and frustration is justified.

Whenever you get angry with someone, don't judge yourself for the anger, but be compassionate with yourself and figure out a way to release the anger. When you notice rage, sadness, disappointment, depression or addiction, be aware that these negative emotions are trying to tell you to spend some time with your inner child. These negative emotions are indicative that your childhood wounds are showing.

Reactions

Sometimes in your life you will have an unrealistic, over-the-top negative reaction to what is really just a simple disagreement with another person. That unrealistic adverse reaction is often heartbreaking and makes you feel terrible about who you are. It doesn't feel good when you get so angry you feel like you're going to implode. When you have a negative reaction to something someone does or says to you, you should pay attention to that reaction because it reveals sorrow, which is usually from your childhood. The source of your explosive reaction to a minor infraction against you is from violations in your childhood. Those emotional reactions to the current scenario have nothing to do with your current scenario but are rooted in your childhood. They have to do with a time when your inner child was so overwhelmed that it felt no sense of control. Your inner child becomes terrified of what it considers to be abuse, and reacts adversely to it. When you were little you had absolutely no control over the mental, emotional, or physical infractions against you. As an adult, your inner child wants to be able to finally *stop* the abuse.

Last week, I was having cable Internet installed in my house, when I had one of those unrealistic emotional reactions. When it came time for them to leave, the installers wanted to collect C.O.D. per their instructions from their office. When I arranged for the installation, I was told by the company representative that I would *not* have to pay C.O.D. When they told me I needed to give them a check I felt and then reacted with rage. I was livid. I paid them but was still furious. After they left I needed to tune in to my inner child to see how having the cable guys want money upset her. I did that because I consciously realized that I had no realistic reason to become that angry. My inner child was so upset because someone went back on his or her word. She felt powerless to fight back, there was nothing she could do and she felt she had been lied to. Because I had that realization I was able to speak with her to help her to feel powerful. I stood up for her by stating categorically that I was *not* happy with their business practice. It made my inner child feel better and comforted that someone stood up for her. I was able to immediately release that anger from my cellular memory because I understood its source.

Lately, I have been going through a tremendously difficult emotional time. My inner child has been horribly upset and rearing her wounded head in many situations – not just with the cable company. My inner child's hurt feelings got triggered a couple of weeks ago when I was meeting with a production company about a television show. I was there to sell myself in order to be on one of their television shows featuring intuitives. While I was waiting in the lobby for the interview I felt the panic starting to swell internally. I heard the thoughts of my inner child crying out, "Who am I? I don't know who I am; how should I act?" Little Pammie, my inner child, was terrified of not only being criticized, but also of being showcased for what she could do. When I was a child my father judged me so harshly for my abilities to speak with divine messengers that when I was faced with the prospect of being judged for my abilities, my inner child freaked out. She was terrified of showing these unknown people her abilities to hear and see spirits.

As a child, I was never allowed to talk about my experiences with my so-called imaginary friends. It was considered taboo as well as impossible for me to talk to God or Jesus because I was a little girl. According to my family's religious beliefs, little girls could never talk to God directly, because male ministers were the only ones allowed to have a conversation with God. After my mother died I used to sit outside on my families front porch and talk to her. My family thought I was crazy and I got in a lot of trouble for doing it. They thought that I was delusional because I wasn't just talking to her; I was having full on conversations with her. It was then that I learned to ignore my ability to speak with spirits because it got me into deep trouble. With their limited consciousness they were convinced it was the devil speaking to me. I didn't want the devil to talk to me, so I tried to stop letting any spirits communicate.

After that television meeting I became overwhelmed with emotions. I couldn't stop shaking and freaking out. I couldn't let go of the damaging emotional onslaught from the sheer terror of being judged. I hated the way I acted in the interview as well as being critical of everything I said. By the time I got home I was crying so hard I had to lie down. I curled up in the fetal position for hours, unable to even talk to anyone about it. I didn't know what fear had surfaced, but I knew it was going to be an amazing opportunity for growth. After I got to a place where I could talk about it, I called a therapist friend for help. Thanks to her amazing intuitive ability to see my inner child, we were able to get to the source of the panic. We worked with little Pammie until she was able to disclose her real fears. Turns out she still had tremendous pain over being abused. The possibility of judgment triggered the judgment and abuse she endured. All the work I've done on healing from within was still not enough for her. She still felt that no one had been there to protect her from the abuse and judgment.

I was shocked that such intense pain was still stored in my cells. I had heard mental professionals talk about inner child work, but I've never felt such tremendous, intense, excruciating pain. I've never gotten to the place where I could see and feel my little girl's pain experientially. Thanks to my enhanced ability to pay attention and my friend's skills as a therapist, I was able to literally go back in time and experience the actual suffering of my inner child. I knew in that moment that little Pammie was getting her just attention. Since that day I have recognized when Pammie needs attention and I make sure I give it to her. Whenever she needs to cry, I let her. After that initial release I have had about four more episodes of releasing the excruciating wounds of my childhood. Even though I have been aware of the need for inner child work, I have never been able to heal experientially. I have never felt that everyone needed therapy to help them get to their internal wounds. After last week, I changed my mind. I now realize how essential therapy with the right therapist can be. My deep, intense healing last week could probably not have happened if it weren't for working with my therapist. We all need help from time to time, so don't hesitate to get it if you need it. Healing your soul is the most important priority of your life, so please take the time to take care of your inner child.

Lost childhood

Thanks to the onslaught of information on the Internet and television, children today are being robbed of their childhood. Out of financial necessity both parents are forced to work to pay their bills and leave their kids to fend for themselves. This lack of a childhood guarantees a wounded childhood. As a child, you need your parents' love and support in order to love yourself. When you don't get that support it creates wounds, those caused by a lack of love. From the very first moment you do not feel loved by your parents, a wound is created. Those wounds are what cause young people and adults to act out in order to get attention. It doesn't matter if that attention is good or bad, just that they are getting attention. By the time young people are fifteen years old they experience life events that were once held at bay until much later. Children today have smoked, drank, and had sex before they can even drive, so by the time they are of so-called *legal age* they've done it all. They do this because they are trying to bury the hurt of their wounded soul.

    Teens don't act out because they feel *good* about their lives; they act out because they don't. Teens, as well as adults, drink, smoke, and do drugs to cover up their pain – not celebrate it. They try to pretend that they're having such a great time, but what they are doing is piling on the pain of their childhood with guilt. Didn't you? Did you do things as a youngster, teenager or young adult that you still have guilt about? I guarantee the answer is yes. That guilt is piled on top of the wounds of your childhood; they are stored in your cells and need to be released. All the negative actions of your teenage and young adult years are because of the abuse to your inner child. If you are an alcoholic as an adult, it's partially because you have guilt about your actions as a teenager and young adult, and this is because of the unresolved emotions of your inner child. The wheels go round and round until you get a flat tire. In order to put air back in the tires, you need to heal the guilt of your childhood, teenager and young adult. To stop the destruction, you need to be able to forgive yourself by understanding your self-destructive behavior.

Cyclical life

Your soul has an innate *need* to have negative experiences, in order for you to heal the negative experiences of your past lives – your karma. Your soul needs to learn to love itself no matter your ostensible mistakes, no matter the lifetime. The soul never forgets. As a human being you do *stupid* things and every time you do you judge yourself then love yourself less, which makes you make more mistakes, which makes you love yourself less. Self-loathing is cyclical.

Healing the kid inside

To heal the inner child takes time, compassion, and patience. Healing the inner child requires you to always pay attention to it. The inner child needs love and understanding because it feels like it has never received love and understanding. He or she needs to know that no matter what, you will love him or her. In order to heal your inner child, you must treat it as a separate entity. You must treat it differently from how your parents treated you or you are as guilty as they are of abusing you. You must treat yourself with loving kindness for healing to take place.

As an adult, your mind is jaded with an agenda, which has been influenced by the belief system of your parents. In order to mend the damage inside, you must first remember the pain *as* the inner child, to acknowledge how intense his or her pain really was. As an adult your perception of the trauma you experienced is that of an adult, but you forget that when you were little your perception and suffering was much more intense. You had no reasoning ability to think, "My parents did the best they could." As a child you don't understand that your parents were the ones that either intentionally or inadvertently did unloving things to you.

To help you heal, you should remember how badly you felt when your parents told you to shut up and go to your room. Try to remember your thoughts about life when you were little. Remember the times you had great ideas but your parents never let you express them. Remember the frustration you felt when your parents harshly punished you for something that was normal for a kid. Do you remember how brilliant you were before someone told you that you weren't? These are just mild incidences of how your parents screwed with your self-esteem and self-love. Just imagine how badly you were harmed when there was intense physical, mental, or emotional abuse. Those afflictions are not easily thought away. Those deeply invasive, horrific, life-changing events are stored in your cellular memory as a lack of love. Those afflictions are not resolved until you take action to resolve them. By remembering your negative experiences you can begin to unlock the hidden torment of the little kid inside you. You have to know that your inner child has just cause to be upset and emotional. You have to remember the actual pain, not the adult memory of the pain.

Here are a few simple things you can do to help your inner child heal. But remember, if you are experiencing extreme trauma in your life, go and see a mental professional for help.

1. Make a list

Divide a piece of paper into three columns. In the first column make a list of five of the most painful moments of your life. In the second column list how those painful moments made you feel; be as specific as possible. In the third column, write down the dialogue your parents used during those moments. Remembering their words is crucial in helping you overcome your pain. After making the list, slowly analyze it; think about what it felt like to be in those moments. Then say this mantra, " Well, no wonder I didn't feel loved."

You can take this one step further by continuing to say the mantra several times a day. Your conscious mind must come to the realization that you have a reason to be f'd up. You must consciously recognize that you have a reason to be upset about your life. In order to heal, your inner child needs to know that it has just cause in feeling unloved.

2. Talk to her/him

Perform a ritual that involves your inner child. Close your eyes and imagine sitting down on a park bench with the child inside of you. Talk to her and tell her how much you love her. Tell her she never did anything wrong. Tell him how proud you are of him. Once you've done this, give yourself a big hug. Tell your inner child that you will always be there for her. Tell him that no one will ever hurt him again because you won't tolerate it. Tell her you'll protect her. All your inner child has ever wanted was to be loved. Spend some time with your inner child and do just that. Treat him or her like you wish your parents had treated you.

3. Have playtime

Most of us are forced to grow up way too fast. You're wounded by such an early age, that you don't have time to enjoy your youth. As an adult you can choose how you spend your days, so spend some of them having fun. Play with child-like innocence and abandon. Go to a playground and slide down a slide. Have a friend push you on a swing. Ride a merry-go-round. Do anything you enjoyed as a child, only this time, let go of all your pain and just enjoy the ride. As a child, you play to express your creativity and joy, but when your childhood is filled with abuse you lose that creativity and joy. Playing as an adult helps you get it back.

4. Pay attention

Your inner child needs you to notice him/her. He or she needs to be sad, angry, and afraid and you need to notice when he or she is. Take the time to understand why she, and therefore you, feel that way. The inner child reacts when he or she is upset. He or she reacts by being defensive, aggressive, or sad. Any time you feel that way your inner child is crying out for help and when he or she does, take the time to talk to him or her and work it out. When you notice your inner child reacting emotionally, write down what caused the reaction. Almost every negative emotional response can be traced back to a childhood incident, so find it and you will be able to figure out why you are the way you are.

With time and attention, your inner child can be healed. So please, pay attention to him or her; talk and play with him or her. If you will take the time to work on the issues of the child inside, your personal relationships as well as your world will massively improve.

8
YOUR SUBCONSCIOUS MIND: YOUR PROTECTOR

Your mind consists of three parts: the conscious, the subconscious, and the higher consciousness. The conscious mind allows you to function on a daily basis. You use it to perform your daily routines such as paying bills, doing your job, taking care of your children, etc. The conscious mind is the rational, thinking part that filters right and wrong. The higher consciousness is the all-knowing aspect of your mind. The higher consciousness is divine intelligence that has no need to learn. It only needs to remember that it already knows everything. In order for you to access your higher consciousness, the conscious mind must break through the barriers of the subconscious to create a pathway to the higher consciousness. You incarnate to face and resolve the fears of the subconscious.

Some consider the subconscious the saboteur. I consider the subconscious mind a loving protector with an ironclad memory; it *never* forgets a fear. As far as the subconscious mind is concerned, everything that has ever happened to you is happening right now. It knows no space or time and remembers all wounds, from any point in this lifetime or another, until they are healed. Its job is to protect you. If the subconscious feels you have ever experienced pain from a particular situation it will do everything in its power to protect you from repeating that situation. Because its job is to protect you from repeating that situation it will pull out all stops to do that job. For example, if you were a singer in a past life that fell to your death from a stage, your subconscious mind would do everything in its power to prevent you from performing on stage in this lifetime because of the fear of dying. In this life you might still want to be a singer, but the fear in your subconscious of dying will block it from happening. Try as you might to achieve that goal it will seem like you are being sabotaged at every turn. In order to overcome this, you must overcome the fear of your subconscious.

The subconscious is also our protector when it comes to karmic relationships. A karmic relationship is one in which you have such a strong connection with someone that no matter how hard you try, or how painful the relationship might be, you just can't break away from it. Have you ever been in love with someone who was abusive, yet you just couldn't bring yourself to leave them? Have you ever felt completely paralyzed to leave a relationship that you knew in your heart wasn't good for you? That is the protective subconscious mind controlling the conscious mind so that you can heal the karma before you break away. I will talk more about karmic relationships in the chapter on past lives, but if you would delve deeper into the karma of an unhealthy relationship, you would be able to leave that relationship. Walking away from a difficult relationship is easy once you heal the karma.

The subconscious mind is where fear is manifested. Fear in the subconscious is what immobilizes you in moving forward in your life. The subconscious keeps you from fulfilling your hopes and dreams as long as you allow it to dominate your life. So, how can the subconscious mind be your protector when it protects you from the good things you want in your life? Well, because the subconscious doesn't think it's harming you. Its perspective is one of protection. In order to heal, you must convince your subconscious that you're safe in having what you want. This takes repetition. You must repeatedly tell it that you are in control and this is a new experience and that the old one no longer applies. You must repeatedly tell your subconscious what to think in order to adjust its pattern of thought that is dictated by past experiences. Because the subconscious knows no space or time, it thinks you're still experiencing the pain from a past life or your childhood; it doesn't realize that the current moment is the only one that is real. You must use your conscious mind to tell the subconscious that this moment is different. Tell the subconscious in those single moments of fear that you are safe and not afraid. Doing so will help you run your life consciously, rather than letting the subconscious run your life through fear. For most people in the world, the subconscious mind is in charge eighty-five percent of the time. You act and react on the fears of the subconscious, and your conscious mind doesn't step in and say, "Hey, knock it off, we're fine!"

Because fear comes from the cellular memory of the subconscious, you must pay attention to and then identify your fears. Let's say you have an unrealistic fear of heights, yet nothing has happened in your life to cause you to be afraid of heights. That's your subconscious mind reliving in this moment what happened in another. It's desperately trying to keep you from getting hurt. The same goes for all phobias, be they of the dark, spiders, water, or enclosed spaces. At their core, they're all the same thing – the subconscious trying to keep you from re-experiencing pain or death by making you fearful.

On a recent trip to a spa, I had the opportunity to face one of my phobias: drowning. This fear has kept me from having any kind of fun around water. I was determined to overcome this phobia that had plagued me my entire life. I would freak out in pools if someone splashed water on my face, while snorkeling, or swimming in the ocean. During the *water dance* (a ritual of massaging a person while in a shallow body of water), I freaked out when the therapist turned my face into the water. When he touched the back of my neck to turn me over into the water, it literally felt as if someone was putting their hands on the back of my head to drown me. I had a subconscious cellular reaction to the current moment. Even though my conscious mind knew this gentleman would never harm me in any way, my subconscious didn't know the safety of the therapist; all it knew was the danger from a drowning of the past. Consciously knowing that it was a subconscious cellular reaction still did not help me to overcome my fear of drowning. My resolution was that I may never be able to overcome that fear, so I have to accept that as my reality. You need to be able to accept wherever you are in life. I accept that I have that fear and have joy that I haven't drowned in this lifetime.

Your subconscious mind reveals to you what you're thinking through your feelings and actions. Some signs that your subconscious is filled with fearful thoughts are disease, addiction, and sabotage. The negative thoughts of your conscious mind are enough to create disease and addiction, but coupled with the subconscious' need to protect you, it can be a seemingly overwhelming task to heal yourself.

Disease

When you come to the realization that you're a soul first and a body second, you will begin to understand why your body gets sick. Your body creates disease when your soul doesn't feel loved. At your core you are nothing but pure love, so when your thoughts about yourself aren't loving ones, you are in conflict with your true nature and you get sick. You then manifest physical or mental disorders. The sick body shows you your thoughts and reveals what you're thinking about yourself. Your energy flows according to your loving thoughts and when you don't have enough of them, your energy stops flowing and you get sick. *Dis-ease* is when the soul is literally not at ease. Louise Hay has a wonderful book, *You Can Heal Yourself*. It explains what each sick body part means from the soul's perspective. It will help you understand what your ill body is trying to tell you.

Addiction

In our society, people with addictions are often judged harshly. You look at their lives and assume it should be easy for them to stop drinking, doing drugs, eating so much, shopping so much, etc. You wonder how a mother could choose to drink herself to sleep each night instead of spending quality time with her children or how a father would rather be at a bar than his son's baseball game. They drink because their souls hurt. They hate themselves so much the only way they can cover their pain is to numb it. Further exacerbating the problem is their judgment about the numbing practices. They know it's wrong and that knowledge causes them to drink more. Addiction indicates self-hatred. From food to cocaine, an addiction indicates the soul is hurting, so hating yourself for being addicted just creates more addiction. To truly stop an addiction, you must stop judging, show compassion and get to the root of the pain – that thing that caused you to start the addiction in the first place. Sometimes that source is from a past life; sometimes it's from childhood but regardless of what it is, it should be noted that it's always a trigger for the subconscious. The subconscious immediately remembers the previous pain and equates the two.

While there are many types of addictions, the themes are the same. I want to focus on two that I feel are most pervasive at this time.

The first is drug or alcohol addiction. People think that extensive partying is a way to express themselves. They convince themselves that drunken antics are fun, but they never really are. It's an illusion. What they are really doing is covering up their internal agony. Don't get me wrong; I'm not a teetotaler and I'm not saying there's something wrong with a drink or two; rather, I'm talking about excessive drinking. When someone continuously drinks himself or herself into a drunken stupor, something is wrong inside. It's not a celebration; it's a disguise. By partying you are trying to show the world that everything is good in your life, when it isn't. While the world might be fooled, your soul never is; the subconscious never is. You can never run from your truth. The suffering will continue to surface until you stop running and allow yourself to discover the source of it. You must face your fear.

Food addiction is also very common. Although it is seemingly not as devastating to society as drugs or alcohol, it can be devastating to you. A sad woman and a carton of Ben and Jerry's are so commonplace it has become a clichéd joke. Well, a food addiction is this on a greater scale; it just isn't funny. If you over consume you are either trying to fill a void or are trying to *not* be noticed by others. The void you are trying to fill is most often caused by a lack of love in your childhood. For some it is because of physical abuse.

For others it's from mental or emotional abuse. The soul records that abuse as a lack of love, and you fill that void with food. You eat sweets or other comfort food because your wounded spirit needs to feel comforted and food is the way to feel nurtured.

Overeaters don't love themselves enough for the world to see. For whatever reason, if you are an overeater, you do not want to be noticed so you try and be someone the world would choose not to look at. You eat to cover up your wounds. I've been guilty of it myself. I've been terrified of being noticed, so I've over-eaten, over-indulged, and under exercised. Now, why would I do that? Why would I not want to be noticed? What was the fear in my subconscious driving this behavior? The fear is of having someone notice me and want to be with me. What would happen if someone were to notice and – God-forbid – love me? I finally figured out that I'm not really afraid of the actual love, I'm afraid of myself when I love someone. I lose myself in my lover's wants and needs. I set what I want aside and focus on my partner. In every relationship, I sacrificed myself in order to fulfill my partner's needs thus ignoring my own. I did this because I didn't value me. My subconscious had worked really hard to convince me that in order to be safe I needed to be unattractive.

Sabotage

In Marianne Williamson's book, *Return to Love,* she eloquently explains the soul's desire to cover up its light:

> "Our deepest fear is not that we are inadequate. Our deepest fear is that we are powerful beyond measure. It is our light, not our darkness that most frightens us. We ask ourselves, who am I to be brilliant, gorgeous, talented, fabulous? Actually,

who are you not to be? You are a child of God. Your playing small does not serve the world. There is nothing enlightened about shrinking so that other people won't feel insecure around you. We are all meant to shine, as children do. We were born to make manifest the glory of God that is within us. It's not just in some of us; it's in everyone. And as we let our own light shine, we unconsciously give other people permission to do the same. As we are liberated from our own fear, our presence automatically liberates others" (pages 190–191).

I had a client who wanted to overcome being lazy at work. His office was a mess and he refused to clean it up. He was in constant trouble with his boss for his sloppy work environment. No matter how much he really consciously wanted to clean it up, he couldn't, even though he knew his job might be in jeopardy. In one of our sessions, he discovered that his subconscious mind was so afraid that he would actually stay at that job; it was protecting him by sabotaging his ability to be tidy, which in effect would cost him his job. His real passion was writing, but he convinced himself he had to have his computer job to pay the bills. He thought that being creative would keep him from being able to earn a living. For years his family told him writing was a silly pipe dream. All of this contributed to him working in a more *secure career* that he hated, but his subconscious *knew* he didn't want to be a computer tech, so it tried to help him become a writer by creating a situation in which he might lose his secure career. After several sessions of working on this fear, he took the leap and went after a job that was more creatively fulfilling.

I've had a personal experience with sabotage just while writing this book. My subconscious has done everything it could to keep me from finishing it. In many past lives,

I was persecuted for speaking about the spiritual truth of life. For me to now write my truth on paper for all to see – well, you can imagine the hoops my subconscious began jumping through! In order to keep me from writing this book, which it equated with my eventual persecution, my subconscious experienced pangs of terror at the thought of being recognized, so I would stop writing. My fears convinced me that I was too old and fat for anyone to care about what I had to say. Those judgments and fears had me sitting on my sofa and eating Mochi Ice Cream. It told me I was too stupid to write, so I threw away pages that might have had substance. But, in the end, through the process, I began to realize that I had to live what I was writing. In practicing what I was preaching, I decided that no matter what happened, I was going to write this book. I stared at my subconscious and the fears long buried there and I said "F'it. I'm going to finish this book!" And I did – and I'm still alive. I paid attention to my fears and then I rejected them. This is exactly what it takes to overcome the protective nature of the subconscious. By changing the conscious thoughts to overrule the subconscious, the higher conscious is allowed to shine.

Healing the subconscious

As I stated earlier, the subconscious mind is in control about eighty-five percent of the time. People consciously think what their subconscious mind is telling them to think. When you're afraid, no matter what it is that you're afraid of, it is coming from your subconscious. The only exception to that is when the fear is coming because your intuition is telling you there is a legitimate threat to your safety. Sometimes it's difficult to differentiate subconscious fear from intuition and the best way is to really pay attention to the fear. Is it recurring? Have you always been afraid of flying or are you sick to your stomach about this particular flight? You will know the difference based on how you feel at the time. If your stomach is all tied in knots and your entire body is saying, "No, do not get on that plane," then it is your higher conscious and intuition at work, and I would suggest honoring it by not getting on the plane. But if you are normally nervous about flights, then go ahead and fly. When I was on a sabbatical in Peru a few years ago, I was planning on staying for a few more weeks until one morning I woke up with this fearful need to get out of Peru as quickly as I could. I had a strong intuitive feeling that I must get home. I was sick to my stomach, terrified of not getting home as soon as possible. I felt like if I didn't leave immediately, I might not be able to get out of there. I got up, got dressed and immediately went to a local travel agent to change my flight to return home early. When I called my daughter to tell her I was coming home, she asked me why I would cut my trip short. All I could tell her was that I was afraid of staying there and I had to come home immediately. I arrived home on September 9, 2001 – two days before the 9/11 attacks. Had I not trusted my fearful intuition, I would not have been able to get home for quite a while. My fearful gut told me that I needed to be home before the attack.

Your intuition will feel like a *knowing*, not a panic attack. Once you practice paying attention to these subtle differences, you will find it easier to tell the difference between your subconscious fears and your higher-conscious knowing.

Here are a couple of suggestions for helping you overcome your fearful subconscious thoughts.

1. Notice body language
Your body language is a big part of your intuition.
The reaction of your body shows you your fears.
Your reaction tells you when something is amiss

internally. If you get knots in your stomach or a pain in your chest, you need to acknowledge them. If your stomach hurts, it's because there's something in your life you literally can't stomach. Let that throbbing headache show you that you should be feeling more and thinking less; that you should be thinking of yourself as a soul with a body, not a body with a soul. Your subconscious mind talks to you through your body. When you're afraid – whether it is a phobia or a fear of falling in love again – your subconscious tells you through your body. Listen to it. Pay attention when it hurts and you can stop it from hurting.

2. Repeat after me

The subconscious mind needs repetition. It needs to be told over and over again that it has no reason to fear. You cannot expect your fears to magically disappear unless you repeatedly acknowledge them. Every single time a fear surfaces, recognize it and change the thought. Do this over and over again until you heal the fear. *Get in the game!* Repeat to yourself that you have no reason to be afraid. If you need to use a mantra, then use a mantra. Repeat to yourself, "I am safe flying" whenever you board a plane. Then, after you safely exit the plane, say it again and celebrate how safe you were. Remember to energetically express joy about your new thoughts of being safe. In addition to changing the thought, you have to change the emotion from a fearful one to a joyous one. When you do this your subconscious mind will release your fear.

9
THOUGHTS ARE THINGS

I'm sure you've heard the saying, "Thoughts are things," many times, but chances are the concept hasn't completely resonated with you because you view yourself as physical. The negative thoughts in the Universe cause the world to be ostensibly f'd up. The negative thoughts create a negative world, which makes you think the world is f'd up, which makes you have negative thoughts about the world, which creates a negative world because of your negative thoughts. Negativity is cyclical.

You rationalize your existence based on looking at yourself and everything else in the Universe as physical realities. Yet, physical life is an illusion; it isn't real. The reality is that in order to understand the f'd up nature of the world you must go beyond the physical and embrace the concept that thoughts are what create and define your existence. The Universe, or God, if you will, is thought. Thought is God.

Your energy is comprised of millions of thoughts. When you are in pain it is because of your thoughts. Hell truly is a state of mind, a state of thoughts. However you think you are; you are. If you think you are happy, you will be happy. If you constantly think about negative or unhappy things, you will be negative and unhappy. From the body to the mind to the spirit, we are nothing but thoughts. If you're sitting on a sofa now reading this book, someone first thought about the sofa; then they built it from the fabric and wood derived from someone else's thoughts. Everything in this Universe is based on thoughts.

Your think tank is designed to do just that: think. You not only have your own thoughts to deal with, but you also have to deal with the thoughts of others. Your subconscious literally picks up the thoughts of others and makes them your own. Anytime you come into the aura of others you can pick up their thoughts and misinterpret them as your own. Sometimes you will feel depressed when you really aren't because you are picking up the thoughts of a friend or even a disincarnated spirit that is depressed. Whenever someone is within your aura you are capable of picking up his or her thoughts. Whenever you unconsciously pick up on the negative thoughts of others, your conscious mind tries to rationalize the thoughts, and then turns them into the emotions of those thoughts. If you just spoke with a friend who is sad, you will pick up on those thoughts and become sad, then your conscious mind tries to rationalize why it is sad; it frantically tries to find a reason for the sadness. It will then choose a part of your life and assign the sadness to it, thereby making it your sadness.

Ever walk into a friend's or stranger's home and feel a drop in your energy and wonder why? It's because you are feeling the thoughts in that house. Ever go into a restaurant and just want to turn around and leave? That's the negative thoughts of the employees and other patrons. You know the feeling of being in a place that has negative thoughts or energy. It's uncomfortable or even creepy just to be there. For example, one day I was meeting my friend Stephanie at this cute little coffee house in Santa Monica. From the outside, it seemed so charming. But immediately upon entering, I felt sick to my stomach. When I expressed this to Steph, she asked me if I knew what the building used to be. Of course I didn't, but once I tuned in, all I could feel was death. She then explained to me the cute, charming little coffee house had previously been a meat packing plant where animals were slaughtered. There had been several other businesses that tried establishing successful businesses in this location, yet failed. Why? Because people unconsciously picked up on the pain and the panic within the former slaughterhouse so they didn't want to patronize the business. It wasn't until the place became a new coffee house, a haven for creative types who made it their home, that the energy was eventually changed.

There is a reality of energetic thoughts that you don't recognize because you can't see it; but you're feeling it. Unconsciously, you pick up on the thoughts of other people's energy whether they're dead or alive. You can pick up on thoughts that are psychic impressions along with your own subconscious fears. Several years ago, a friend and I were driving to a party. Once we parked and exited the car, I was immediately nauseous. I couldn't move and had knots in my stomach. I told my friend I had a really bad feeling and that I didn't think we should go to the party because of the dark energy surrounding this place. She let me know we weren't in any danger, we just happened to be parked in front of where Nicole Brown Simpson's condo used to be. We were there a year after the horrific murders took place, yet the energy and thoughts remained so strong, they chilled me to the bone. I can't imagine how I would have felt after that experience if I didn't have the ability I have to understand it. Imagine how difficult it is to keep a clear mind with all those negative thoughts and impressions out there that can jump into your existence at any time. It's no wonder people sometimes think they're going crazy!

When you meet a confident, secure, happy person, you immediately feel it. You say they have good energy, and I am saying that good energy comes from how they think about themselves. If you're secure in your thinking, you're secure in your life, literally. Yet, if you meet someone who just got dumped by their girlfriend of six years, you would feel the unhappiness and think they had bad energy. Unfortunately, you may also think they are upset with you, not knowing how to process what you're interpreting. You take what they are experiencing personally; begin to feel bad about yourself, which then gives you bad energy. Ninety percent of the time, if someone appears unhappy, it has to do with something in their life not yours. Because you're a human, you're set on automatic pilot to blame yourself; you take on the responsibility of someone else's bad mood. The best way to counteract that and help a friend heal is to ask them what's wrong. Doing so makes sure you don't take it personally and allow it to affect you. It's a self-esteem saver!

How you feel about yourself is what you think about yourself and that's how the world around you feels about you. Your feelings precede you. Your aura, an energy field that extends about five feet from your body, reveals to people how you're feeling whether you say anything or not. If you're feeling particularly good about yourself one day, you will get positive reactions from everyone you meet; you might find a dollar on the sidewalk, or get an unexpected phone call bearing good news. People will smile at you more; you will sing, laugh and have a great day, because your thoughts are good ones. Because of this, all around you will be positively affected and have better days as well. Similarly, people can tell and treat you differently when you're in a bad mood. If you start off having a bad day and do nothing to change it, you will continue to have things go wrong throughout the day. You'll receive odd reactions from everyone you meet; you might lose a dollar or even get an unexpected phone call bearing bad news. As you expect more things to go wrong in the day, they will.

In order to change your life, you must change the thoughts about your life. I remember days when something went wrong I would say, "What else is going to go wrong?" Then something else would go wrong. It did because I was expecting it to. During that time, I was a financial disaster, healing from a broken relationship, and had a car that was on its last leg. I was physically, mentally, and emotionally broken. I didn't know much, but I did know that nothing was going my way, so I chose to start drinking. While taking that first sip, I thought it would all get better, but drinking made everything worse. I drank away the little extra money I had, which made me more financially and emotionally broken. This cycle was destroying my energy with every thought. I couldn't seem to pull myself out of it until I realized that thinking bad things wasn't working, so I decided to try thinking good things. Slowly, over time, I didn't feel like drinking, my car began obeying and I always had a little extra cash in my bank account.

Thoughts are things means that you are literally creating your life with your thoughts. If you think you are successful, you are. If you think you live in poverty, you do. The creative thoughts of your life are not only in the conscious, but also in the subconscious. I know that the book and movie, *The Secret*, tells you this same thing. It says that if you think of what you want, instead of what you don't want, you will have everything in life that you desire: the big house, the fancy new car, and the love of your life. I basically agree with that philosophy but with an addendum. I don't want anyone to have an unrealistic expectation about getting what he or she wants. If you do the work--visualize the things you want, create positive reactions to everything in your life, change your thoughts, pay attention to all your negative thoughts and change them--but nothing changes in your life, then please don't judge yourself harshly about it. The reason you're not achieving your hopes and dreams is because of the protective subconscious. For you to create the life you want, you *must* clear the fear of having what you want in your subconscious. Your unconscious fears may block those hopeful dreams from becoming a reality. Just don't get mad at yourself and think you're still doing something wrong. Instead, go to a past life therapist or energy healer or intuitive to get some help. You can't fix it if you don't know it's broken!

I had a client who was depressed and angry, claiming that God was standing in her way of having an acting career, beginning a relationship, and having money. She thought God was preventing her from happiness. I suggested she wasn't really mad at God, but at herself for not achieving her goals. After talking for a while, we discovered that her mom and dad always fought over money. They argued about how there was never enough, no matter how hard they worked or what they did. She learned her viewpoint of deprivation from them. It was imbedded in her cells that she would always need for something, and so she did. Once she realized she was reacting to an old pattern that wasn't even hers, she was able to forgive herself for manifesting the lack her thoughts were projecting. She realized God wasn't to blame; her own thoughts were sabotaging her. Some of you might be upset right now, thinking "Well, that's not me! I don't sabotage my life!" If you really think about your life and how your thoughts might be directing it, you will realize how degrading some of them are. You would never be so judgmental with others you love; yet you do it to yourself. To overcome this, you must learn to have loving kindness for the one person in the world that can change your life: you!

Think of life this way: if you're responsible for your bad life, it means you also have the power to create a good life. It means you and you alone can change everything! Isn't it exciting to think that if you just habitually think about how you want your life to be, your life will be that way? I was thrilled when I finally figured this out. I was elated to think that I alone created what I perceived to be my devastating life because it meant that I alone could change it. It meant there wasn't some mysterious, omnipresent entity pulling the strings; I didn't need to pray for help then wait for it; I didn't have to love God more, go to church more, or do anything outside myself. Finally, I had hope, which you should have too. Inside of everyone is the power to change his or her life. You don't have to rely on anyone but yourself in order to achieve it. Again, you do not have to rely on an all-powerful force to change your life because you are the all-powerful force. You just need to pay attention to what you're thinking and change negative patterns. Loving thoughts conquer all.

Single thought therapy

Single thought therapy is a method by which you can rid yourself of negative thoughts one thought at a time. By paying attention to each individual negative thought and then changing those negative thoughts, you can change your reality. It takes a constant state of awareness to change each individual thought, but you can learn to do it. Whenever you have a negative thought about yourself, simply tell yourself that you no longer think that way, and then replace that negative thought with a positive one. Replace it with a thought that makes you feel good about yourself. Thinking, "I am beautiful," makes you feel so much better than thinking, "I am ugly," so why not think you're beautiful? Since you have a choice in the thoughts you have, why not think something that makes you feel good instead of something that makes you feel bad?

Single thought therapy is the difference between reacting and creating. I read somewhere once that the difference between those two words is the letter "c". It depends on how you "c" things, whether you re-act or create. If you change each negative thought when it occurs you will eventually run out of negative thoughts.

Single thought therapy makes it easier to pay attention to your thoughts. When you get into the mind frame of only paying attention to one thought at a time, the chaos of the mind is contained. You get back in control of the way your mind works. You're taking charge of your subconscious insanity. You then consciously make choices, instead of making them out of the fear of the subconscious.

Single thought therapy keeps you focused on the present moment and out of the past moments. If you have recently had your heart broken and the mere mention of his name sends you into a deep, dark, weeklong depression, you need *single thought therapy.* By paying attention to the fact that his name makes you hurt, you have the opportunity to change the way you think. Oh, I know you're thinking, "That's easy for her to say, she's not the one with the broken heart." Healing a broken heart works the same way as healing any other type of pain. You need to replace those hurtful hateful thoughts about yourself with loving thoughts for yourself. You must learn conscious kindness for yourself. Remember: one thought at a time. When you catch yourself thinking about him and it hurts, then stop thinking about him and start thinking about something that makes you feel good instead. Think about someone else who loves you; think about your animals; think about the ocean; think about anything that makes you happy.

Single thought therapy is simply changing one negative,

unwanted thought into a positive thought. You can only fix what you notice is broken. This will take practice but it is well worth the effort.

Healing your thoughts

In order to change your life from f'd up to peaceful, you must first think and feel the life you want and do it habitually. You have habitually thought about what you don't want long enough; don't you think it's time to habitually think about what you do want? The more you thought about not having enough money to pay your bills, the more bills you got. The more you thought about not having the perfect relationship, the more rejection you experienced. The more you thought about how you couldn't afford a new car, the more money went out the window. Along with negative thoughts come negative emotions. They go hand in hand to create miserable lives. Whatever you feel passionately about, you create. How about feeling passionately about creating a happy life? Think about what you want with joy; then go about creating it, with joy.

If you want a new healthy relationship, imagine the character of the person you want. Write it down. Write everything that you'd enjoy in another human being. Then go back down the list and feel what it would be like to experience living your life with that person. Take the time to joyously celebrate having a positive loving relationship. That's it, two simple steps. They work in every facet of your life. You want a new car. Write down exactly what you want in a new car. Feel yourself driving it, cut out pictures of it and hang them on your wall. You want a new career? Write down what you want out of a career. See and feel yourself in it. Don't question it, just feel joyful knowing it's yours and it will be. You just have to change the way you think about the things you want.

Here are a few simple steps to changing thought processes:

1. You can't fix it if you don't know it's broken

This simply means, pay attention to your thoughts. You can only change your thoughts if you know what they are! Listen so you will hear and recognize the negative and destructive ones in order to reverse them. You can also pay attention by noticing your body's reaction to what other people say or do. Your physical reaction will give you direct information as to how you're feeling. Knots in the stomach, tightening of the chest muscles, and nervousness are all signs there is a wrong thought in your mind. Pay attention to them, so you can alter those thoughts.

2. Change the thought

In order to end the cycle of negative thoughts, you have to change them one by one. It's like the old joke, "Doctor, it hurts when I do this." The doctor responds, "Then don't do that." When you discover a negative thought, immediately replace it with a new positive one. Instead of thinking "I'm so broke," think "Money flows easily to me." Rather than thinking, "What else can go wrong?" think, "Things are great in my life and I can't wait to experience more of the good things that are on their way!" If what you're thinking doesn't make you feel good, then simply stop thinking it and think something that does. You have a choice. Slowly but surely you will change the way you think and with repetition, you can change all your negative thoughts to positive ones. You'll be amazed how quickly your life changes.

3. Feel differently

Thoughts, along with passion, create our worlds. If you passionately think about something with emotion long enough, you will create it, be it good or bad. If you hate your job and it keeps you up at night because you aren't being appreciated or a co-worker is making you feel miserable, the fix is easy. Rather than staying up thinking of ways to plot revenge, think about how it would feel to love your job and get along with your co-worker. Feel yourself enjoying every moment at your job, and loving every interaction with your co-worker. You might not end up becoming best friends, but your day-to-day interactions will immediately improve. Additionally, you might even find yourself with a better job! Feel yourself holding hands with your perfect mate; feel the ocean breeze against your face as you're on your dream vacation; feel how good it is to have more money than you need to pay the bills. Doesn't it just feel good?

4. Do it habitually

You can't change your life by only thinking new thoughts every once in a while. It must be a daily practice. It must be a ritual. One simple way to achieve this is to create a journal, corkboard, or even refrigerator filled with all the things you want that you know would bring you joy. If you're having a negative thought about something, look at the pictures, the ideas, the images of things you'd like to have. Negative thoughts will immediately be replaced by thoughts of joy and anticipation.

If you want a loving partner, cut out a picture of a happy couple and write your name above it. If it's money you want, tack up a dollar bill and write six zeroes after it. If you want your own new home, flip though magazines until you find the one you know is perfect; then look at it every day. Laugh and smile as you view these images. In your heart feel what it will be like to have them. Be cheerful; do a little dance, the one you will do when you achieve these goals. If cutting out images is not for you, then at least take the time each day to imagine all the good things you want in life and imagine yourself having them.

Make it a habit to say to yourself every day that you love yourself and that you are worthy of all you can imagine. Once or twice a day really won't work; you need to do it four- to five hundred times a day. I know that seems like a lot, but it really takes no more time than it does to drive to the market. Turn off your car radio and tune into yourself. Just remember to make it a habit to love you with passion – and mean it. Do this on a daily basis, while imagining yourself living your most joyful life possible and it will come to you.

You must choose to believe that all your dreams will come true. Hope is not something you have; it's something you choose. Feel giddy. Laugh; jump up and down with excitement at the thought of things to come. There is not some outside obstruction preventing you from attaining all you want. God does not give to some and not to others. The Universe is not keeping score. You are the only thing in the way of your happiness. Make it a habit to focus on your happiness every day; don't wait to be happy.

However, I do have one note of caution about creating a vision board. Remember that we always get what we ask for, so joyously ask for the right things and if some don't come, know there is a Divine reason behind it. Please don't think you're doing something wrong, but instead thank God for unanswered prayers. Just because you get a Mercedes, know that owning that Mercedes does not guarantee true happiness. You must still make yourself happy from within. True happiness comes when you don't need that Mercedes. The vision board you create is just a reminder to you to feel joy. By continuously feeling joy, you manifest more joy.

Also remember that you create opportunities for healing, so just because you got that car of your dreams, you might also get a flat tire while driving it. Life won't be perfect just because you have learned how to manifest. When it happens you must deal with it joyously and realize the Universe is somehow protecting you with the flat tire – it could have saved you from getting into an accident. Don't have unrealistic expectations of perfection and constant pleasure. Ultimately, you are here to heal, so things will always happen that give you that opportunity. Once you commit to habitually loving yourself, you'll find the balance between growth opportunities and having all the things you want for a joyful life. You'll find the degree of difficulty of these experiences will diminish, as well as the time it takes to deal with them.

10
IGNORANCE IS NOT BLISS

You live in a world where your level of personal happiness and peace appears to be based on your external circumstances. You believe that if you could just get everything you think you want and need, you would be happy. If you could only get that new car, bigger home, flat screen HD television set, box seats at Dodger games, or a Trump-esque financial portfolio, then everything would be hunky-dory. Yet, the belief that by merely changing your external circumstances you would create happiness is a false, ego-driven belief. Your ego tells you that joy is something that can only be felt by possessing things or even other people, and if other people envy you having these things then nirvana will follow. It won't. I've met a lot of people with more material possessions than I could ever imagine, yet happiness and peace still elude them.

In order for happiness and peace to be prevalent in

your life, you must stop looking outside for validation and instead look inside to your soul. Happiness and peace truly come from within, not without. The illusion that things and events will bring you happiness is the root of your discontent. Thanks to marketing and advertising geniuses, you have a false expectation that charging that new plasma TV on your Visa card will finally make you feel good about yourself. They've done a brilliant job of convincing the world that those shiny new Jimmy Choo shoes are the direct route to being a happy camper – even if having those shoes means you can't pay your rent. Until you stop focusing on the external, you will never get in contact with the internal, which is the direct route to happiness and peace. Of course, this is not a new philosophy. Mystics and enlightened teachers have been saying this forever. There are hundreds of books that explain the difference between ego and a truly divine life; yet the world is populated with people who still don't understand.

To move from an ego-driven existence to awareness, you must first pay attention to your emotions and come to know the truth of why you're f'd up. You walk around in your pretty new shoes pretending all is well when it isn't. You ignore or accept your inner turmoil, covering it up with the latest pretty frock from the catalog. You seem to think that your pain will magically disappear without spending any time working on your soul. This lack of attention you pay to your emotional self is frightening. How can you ever expect to stop being f'd up when you ignore what is at the center of it, it's *raison d'être*? How can you expect to move forward into a truly blissful life when the majority of your time and energy goes into your home, business, social life, bank account, and gym membership? There's barely enough time left to eat and sleep, let alone make space in the Blackberry for self-awareness. This lack of attention, or attention misdirection, is what causes you to be f'd up.

You've conditioned yourself to believe that if you ignore the pain and fill your life with external sugar coatings the pain will go away. But there's a kicker: ignoring changes nothing. *Ignorance is not bliss.*

You're so afraid to look at the reasons for the tears that you bury them deep inside. Yet, that's why you have the tears in the first place – because you ignore the reasons! In order to heal, you must uncover the source of your hurt. It doesn't just go away by itself. There isn't a magic pill that washes it away. There's no broom large enough that can sweep that pain under the carpet. Hurt will always find its way to the surface. Pain will always make its presence known, one way or another. Those squelched negative emotions that cause you to be f'd up must be addressed, whether it's in this life or another one. So why not take the time now to find out *why* you are *how* you are so you can once and for all end the suffering? If your car has a flat, you immediately call AAA. If a window is broken in your house, you will only live so long with cardboard and duct tape as a solution. Yet, if you cry yourself to sleep every night because you're depressed, you hide it. Why not make your emotional self as important as your car or home. Without you, there'd be nothing to drive or live in! When you focus on your soul's growth, your life immediately changes for the better.

I learned years ago that in order to change my life, I had to change my lifestyle. I began meditating an hour and a half every day without fail. It was hard at first because I was a wife, mother, and professional workingwoman, but I insisted on taking that time for me every day. I told my husband and daughter to give me this time, that I required this time. I didn't allow for any interruptions unless someone was bleeding. This structure brought about a great change in my perspective of life. I became calmer externally because I was calmer internally. I began to understand that I needed to notice me. I began to really be in touch with how I truly felt about things. It brought me more in touch with what my heart was feeling, instead of what my head was thinking. By getting in tune with my soul, I was better able to tune into my life and reap immediate rewards.

So, how does one pay attention to the soul? Quite simply: by paying attention to what you're feeling and acknowledging what you're feeling, you will know what your soul is telling you. Do you spend any time reflecting on your emotional day or do you just accept it as it was? Do you spend the day reacting to the world without noticing the hurt? Do you notice when your heart hurts, when your stomach is in knots or your chest tightens? Are you aware that your body has a negative reaction to the words and actions of others and is an indicator of what your soul is trying to tell you? Become aware. Pay attention. Acknowledge it. Don't judge it. Doing so will allow your truth to surface and as it does, present you with the opportunity to heal. Whenever you feel anything negative, give pause as to the reason behind it. If you feel heaviness in your heart because someone insults you, then you must stop and understand why it hurts you. You will begin to understand that the hurt is coming from your soul, and as you begin to understand that pain, you can begin to overcome it. The easiest way to do this is keep a journal with you. As you feel discomfort, write it down, ask yourself questions, and get to the why of the pain. Write down exactly what was said and done to hurt you, look at it objectively, and listen to yourself. This practice will enable you to become aware of the pain inside that causes you to be f'd up outside.

Okay, so once you notice the pain, what the hell are you supposed to do with it? Great question! Again, you make a choice with every thought you have. You decide whether to continue with those thoughts or create new ones. Re-act or create. Those are your choices and your choice will determine your happiness. Whenever a painful thought occurs, stop and notice it. Then create the positive thought of choice. If you are unable to redirect that particular thought, just smile and choose to remember another time when you weren't feeling this pain; a time when you were experiencing pure happiness. Choose a happy memory when you were loved, when you loved someone else. If you can't think of a memory, spend time with the pet you adore or put on the song that makes you want to crank up the volume, dance, and sing along. After a while, the painful cells and thoughts will be gone, replaced by new joyful ones. Your life is defined by your thoughts, and once you embrace them and stop being ignorant to them, your thoughts – and therefore your life – can change!

Healing the ignorance

Pay attention to your emotional problems. Take time out of every day for your soul. It doesn't matter if it's five minutes or thirty, either will help you heal your problem thoughts in some capacity. It doesn't matter where you start, but once you do, you will immediately begin to notice a difference. This difference will motivate you to spend even more time on your wounds. Once you have gotten into this glorious habit, solving the problems caused by the hidden emotions will be much easier. Ignorance of your soul's pain does not bring you bliss.

Three steps to healing the ignorance:

1. Recognize
Recognize that the pain is trying to tell you something about yourself.

2. Acknowledge
Acknowledge what that something is.

3. Perspective
Change your perspective about the pain. Look at it as an opportunity to heal an old wound.

Once you figure out the source of the problems and understand why you feel so f'd up all the time, and once you grasp why you are how you are, you will be able to create a new, more peaceful you.

11
PAST LIVES AND KARMA

Another reason you are allegedly f'd up is the cellular memory of past lives, or karma. There are varying schools of thought on karma, so it's important to know what it really is before continuing. Many people believe karma is an eye for an eye. If you hurt someone, then you will be hurt. Karma is the Hindu and Buddhist philosophy that the quality of your current and future lives is determined by your behavior in this and previous lives. In other words, you don't get by with anything. The reason you have karma is because we are all one, so what you do to someone else you are actually doing to yourself. Karma is always with the self. There is no one keeping score but you. You are the one that creates retribution for your negative or positive actions. If you hurt someone in this lifetime, your soul remembers that you hurt someone and you want to experience the same pain you inflicted. Why would you want to do that? You do it because at your core, you love everyone. That is what you were designed to do and because of that, you feel the need to experience everything you cause to be experienced. You have an innate need to share the pain. You want to feel what you have caused others to feel. You want to replace the love you took away with love. You want the other person to have the opportunity to return it to you. You want to have emotional experiences, so you would indeed want to have an emotional experience that you created in others. We are all one. We are all from the same source, God. God wants to experience every single emotion, be it negative or positive. So experiencing pain is benefitting and helping God to grow. You are a part of God, so you are designed to grow from pain.

Karma between lives is difficult to understand until you fully grasp that there is no space and time. Karma never forgets what happens in previous lifetimes because the lifetimes are all happening at the same time. Karma remembers everything because it is continuously experiencing everything. As a result of that, and your inherent design, you are a willing participant in karma, whether you recognize it or not. You choose it. If you are in a difficult relationship you can't seem to shake, you can be assured it is a powerful karmic relationship. I had a client who, no matter how hard she tried, she couldn't find the strength to leave a rude, cold, and disrespectful man. Once we discovered that in a past life, she treated him in the same manner, she was able to move on. She learned to forgive herself, love herself and create a new loving relationship with a new man. She recognized the karma and moved on.

Negative karma is not always because you did something harmful to someone in another life; sometimes it's because they did something harmful to you. I have clients who assume that if bad things are happening to them, they must have been a horrible person in a past life. That's not true. Your soul will often return to give other souls an opportunity to feel the pain they have inflicted on you in another lifetime. You will meet up again in your current life and that person will continue to inflict pain on you until you walk away. Your karma was never to stay with that person, but to walk away. Their karma was to stop being cruel.

If someone inflicts harm on you or a family member, you want immediate justice for that action. It's hard to wait for karmic justice, but sometimes you have no choice. That's the only way you'll have true peace in the face of adversity you think was brought to you unjustly. Chances are you may not be around to witness the karmic justice, but you should take comfort in the knowledge it will happen. That is the law of the Universe. When you hear of a killer getting away with murder, you feel for the victim's family. You're angry because it seems that no one is getting restitution. The family may feel like there is no justice in the world. It's excruciating for them to wait for that justice, let alone karmic justice. The way to peace is to remember that Universal justice WILL prevail. A killer will not get away with killing even if they appear to get away with it in this lifetime. Their soul will remember and they will be held accountable either in this lifetime, the afterlife, or the next incarnation.

Three years ago I was living in a house that was contaminated with toxic mold. It was hidden in the walls of the house and my daughter and I had no idea it was there. We became increasingly ill with the passage of time, seemingly without cause. Eventually we discovered the mold and the situation quickly evolved into a major and lengthy legal ordeal. The landlords refused to fix the problem and then illegally evicted us. It was horrible. At one point, before we left the house, I examined potential karmic causes of this chain of events. I wanted to know the reason behind this drama that had suddenly become our lives. I needed to change my perspective about my situation. What I discovered was that in another lifetime our landlords had owned a great deal of property and could be likened to slumlords of today. They were mean, hateful, and would stop at nothing to get what they wanted. At that time, my daughter was married to the landowner's brother. The landowner (our landlord in this lifetime) was jealous of my daughter's husband and the only power he had over him was to control the property we lived in. I was, once again, my daughter's mother who lived in the property with them. The landowner was very angry at his brother for not doing what he wanted and had his henchmen (his wife in this lifetime) burn down the house with all of us in it!

When I saw what was done to my daughter and me in our previous life, I knew what my landlords' karma would be. If, in this lifetime, he did the right thing, fixed the property and allowed us to move back in, all would be well and he would live. But if he didn't do the right thing, he would die, as we did in the previous life. Three months after we were illegally evicted from our home, he died. Three months after that his wife got dementia. They had the opportunity in this lifetime to make up for causing our deaths in a previous life, but when they chose not to do what was right, karmic justice prevailed. I was lucky that because of my intuitive abilities I was able to see the karma from the other lifetime. It helped us to understand and better cope with the craziness we were experiencing, which in turn helped us to release it. But I must say it took over five years for the lawsuit to settle, and I continually had to work on releasing the karma from my soul.

As our souls are in a space-time continuum, they do not recognize the difference between past, present, and future. If you were suffering over anything and did not resolve the pain, then your soul will continue to feel that pain until you resolve it. It makes no difference to the soul if the painful memory happened yesterday or two thousand years ago. It only knows the pain and holds onto it. Your soul is composed of nothing but pure love, and so any fear or emotion that deviates from love causes your soul pain. The anguish your soul experiences is a result of judgment of self. When there is a memory of judgment in your cells you will continue to hurt and repeat the painful pattern until you understand it enough to break it and move on. You do not judge anyone any more harshly than you judge yourself. Until you stop that judgment and start to understand your actions, you will continue returning to those patterns time and time again.

Because I believe in a loving and caring God, I believe in reincarnation. Having more than one shot at perfection would make sense to a loving God. Believing that God would doom you to eternal damnation if you screwed up one time is cruel; God isn't cruel. I believe in reincarnation because I personally had a profound life-healing experience with it. About fifteen years ago I became convinced I was going to die by falling. I was obsessed with it to the point I couldn't leave the house. I was terrified of bridges and would drive twenty miles out of the way to avoid them. I couldn't look at an airplane without having a panic attack and even refused to enter any building over one story. I went as far as to make out a will to ensure my young daughter would be cared for after my impending death. I kept this fear to myself, both embarrassed and terrified of it. Who would believe such random hysteria? At this point I was ready for growth, but had yet to learn about meditation or a spiritual path – let alone reincarnation. The Universe, true to form, sent me what I needed when I was ready.

While attending a broadcasting school, I met a woman who agreed to ride along with me to a job interview about two hours away from my home. Strangely enough, on that drive, she began to talk about reincarnation. She was Catholic, and though Catholicism no longer agrees with the concept of reincarnation, she had a deep belief in it. As she spoke about it, it felt familiar. It made sense to me. It felt like home. I felt as though I knew and agreed with everything she was saying. I was so excited at the prospect of having lived other lives that I questioned her for hours about it. Eventually she suggested I meet with a hypnotherapist friend of hers who could utilize regression to either hypnotize me back to my past lives or she could just see them for me. As soon as I returned from my trip I made an appointment, elated; though when the day of our meeting arrived, I was nervous and frightened. I had no idea what to expect. I watched as she went into a trance and began telling me about another lifetime in which I had been an entertainer. While standing on a ladder to fix a curtain, I slipped and tragically fell to my death at the age of thirty-eight. In this lifetime, I was just thirty days shy of my thirty-eighth birthday! When she came out of the trance, she asked if there was any chance I was afraid of dying. How could she know that? She told me she saw that the death in my previous lifetime was sending my subconscious into a panic because it felt it was in the same situation as before. My subconscious was expecting my body to die. After the reading, I consciously became aware that my fear of death was just that: a fear, not a fact. I could control it, and because I could control it, I banished it. I could cross any bridge I wanted and fly anywhere the skies could take me. It was a miracle; and I knew from that day forward, I was a believer in reincarnation.

I'm thrilled by the idea that we return to our bodies over and over again until we are happy with our journey into the body. I've witnessed the proof of fear based on past lives too many times to count. In sessions with clients, I find that a lot of their problems can be easily explained by examining their past lives. Exploring their past lives also makes sense to my clients, as it explains why they react to certain circumstances the way they do. They begin to see the benefit of the divine plan of reincarnation and how it affects our current lives both positively and adversely. If you're having a fear that seems illogical or unrealistic, a past life therapist can help you witness for yourself the source of that fear. Understanding your karma works better experientially. If you can't find a past-life therapist, you can still heal the fear by understanding that it's not caused by something in the current moment. Once you put it into perspective, you can joyously release it. But remember to be patient, because after a regression or facing a past life fear, it takes time for the conscious body to catch up with the subconscious healing. Just continue to remind yourself that the fear is based in another lifetime and it isn't real. Your subconscious needs repetition. Don't give up!

Healing karma

Healing karma is not an easy task. It takes time, understanding, and dedication. If you don't know of a good past-life therapist, there is only one way to heal and that's through acceptance and love. You must accept the fact that your higher consciousness is determined to heal your wounds. It will continue to put you into negative situations until you resolve your unresolved emotions. You must face each of life's difficult scenarios with a new perspective. You must understand that you are not doing anything wrong by staying with your cruel boyfriend, but you are just trying to heal the karma. You must observe that you are in the difficult situation because you want to learn to love yourself in every situation. You must observe that by staying with this cruel person, you are being cruel to yourself. Learn to love yourself enough to walk away. You don't need to be loved by someone else to feel good. This will give you the strength to walk away and heal the karma. Karma is with the self.

Healing karma means loving yourself, no matter what you've done or are doing. To heal karma you must accept that the reason you do bad things is because you are in pain. Be compassionate with your pain instead of judging it. Accept that you did what you did because you didn't feel loved. Then, love yourself and walk away. The only way to heal karma is through self-love!

12
GROUP CONSCIOUSNESS

For most of this book, I've been discussing personal problems – problems that relate on a small, individual scale. What you need to remember though, is that personal problems saturate the world. Your thoughts literally create and control everything in your physical existence. Your thoughts create everything from your own personal happiness to world peace. With all of us thinking thoughts, we truly are the world. How you feel about your individual world affects how you feel about the world in general, which then affects the way the world feels. Imagine the power in that? Look around right now at your own world. Is it peaceful and joyous? Are you angry and depressed? Those thoughts – negative or positive – permeate everything around you and every thought had by someone else also permeates into your world. Collective thoughts determine the world at large. A world saturated with thoughts of anger, envy, hate, and fear creates natural disasters, military conflicts, and an unstable, unhappy environment. What you need to remember is that the opposite is also true. If you heal the thoughts, you can truly heal the earth.

The connection between mind, body and spirit is never more important than when it comes to world peace. Narcissism has slowly taken the place of civility. Human beings are becoming more narcissistic because they have no sense of power. They feel they have no control of their external world, so they have to fight for some semblance of power. They abuse the rights of others because it makes them feel in control of their lives.

Humankind has become more and more convinced that individual needs outweigh those of humanity at large. Our courtrooms are filled with frivolous lawsuits over the supposed rights of one. Someone doesn't want prayer in school. Someone else doesn't like the flag being flown. Someone else doesn't like revealing pictures of women in a fire station. The list goes on and on, ultimately producing an unproductive, litigious society of selfish indignation. People no longer talk to each other, they talk to lawyers. Why do you no longer care if your actions upset others? How can you ever expect to achieve world peace when you can't even get it with your neighbors? If you ever hope for true world peace, you need to return to civility and remember we truly are all in this together. We are one mind, one body, and one spirit.

How does civility affect world peace? It is directly related to our internal level of happiness. People mistakenly think that by controlling their external world, they will be happy with their internal world. They believe if they get their way, if they get to be right, they will be happy. If you run around doing whatever you want, when you want, without giving a second thought as to who might be adversely affected by your actions, you are adding to the divisiveness of the world.

I'm sure you've experienced a rude neighbor who blares the stereo at all hours of the day and night. Disturbing the peace and quiet of their neighbors is of no consequence to them, yet the consequence they're unaware of is that they're helping create an angry, irritated community that then takes that irritation to the other communities they're a part of. What inevitably happens next is a circle of events that eventually brings negativity back to the rude neighbor, who comes home from work in a bad mood and blares the music to try and feel in control. In reality, a little consideration in the first place would have ended the chain of events. Be considerate if you want others to be considerate of you. Stop and think about how your actions might affect those around you. No one is in this world alone. We all pay the same amount of Universal rent.

Our minds (conscious, subconscious, and higher consciousness) are programmed to always be thinking. We are an amalgamation of thoughts in motion. Your subconscious mind is programmed to think, so if you aren't giving it thoughts, it will reach out and take the thoughts of others. This is so important that you really need to pause and consider it, so I'll repeat it. If you aren't giving your subconscious mind thoughts, it will reach out and take the thoughts of others. When faced with nothing to think about, the subconscious mind will pick up someone else's thoughts and call them its own. Remember, you innately want to heal, regardless of whom is being healed. If you don't think you have anything to worry about, your subconscious mind will take the worries from the person standing next to you at the market and the next thing you know you're worrying about something that in actuality has nothing to do with you. Scary, huh? That's why it is so important to be aware of and in control of your thoughts, so that you'll always know they're yours. And remember – you get to choose which thoughts you want to have. By focusing on your own thoughts, you can make sure you're sending positive, joyful thoughts into the world. Wouldn't you rather have that, knowing you're helping to improve the world, rather than just living with the knowledge that the hostile thoughts of others are influencing it? You create more peace by staying at home and thinking about peace than you do by trying to fight wars.

You live in a world where *group consciousness* is the most powerful ally or enemy you could have. It creates war, peace, and even the weather. If you take a look around you, you'll find most people are living in fear and chaos. They're worried about their careers, their families, and everything they see on the news. When you have the majority of people on the planet filling the Universal thought pattern with these kinds of thoughts, with a group consciousness of negative thoughts, the result is global conflict and natural disasters. Visualize a tornado. It's a dark, swirling cloud of energy. Sounds a lot like a group consciousness of negative fearful thoughts, doesn't it? Know this and you can change this. Just one person changing their part of the group consciousness can shift it. Think, feel, and imagine peace. Others will pick up on your peaceful thoughts, which will overcome their fearful ones and so on. My grandfather had a quaint saying: "shit rolls downhill." One person having a bad day translates into a cavalcade of cranky people walking around, which translates into society as a whole having a bad day. So, how do we fix it? How do we really keep the shit from permanently rolling down the hill?

Healing group consciousness

Everything that has happened, is happening, or will happen is determined by our thoughts. World peace depends upon our peaceful internal thoughts. Some people would vehemently disagree with me, yet I'll say it again. You can never change something by fighting it. Arguing about the Iraq war won't end it, but enough people thinking about it being over will. Whatever you fight against, you create. That's just simple physics; so stop fighting. If you want to stop the war on drugs, stop thinking of it as a war. Why do people do drugs in the first place? They do drugs because they're in pain. No happy person needs drugs – much to the chagrin of some stoners I know. I had a friend who always used to smoke pot before we did spirit channeling, claiming he needed it to help connect with God. Jim Morrison used peyote because he believed it helped him contact people on other planes of existence. He, like my friend, thought a drug would help him connect to God and a world beyond his own. The truth is both my friend and Jim Morrison were using drugs because they were in some way trying to avoid their reality, not connect to a new one. Fortunately, my friend was able to realize this and channel his thoughts into a new direction.

The war on anything will create that which you are fighting. Stop using the words like "fight," "war," and "conflict." Replace them in your thoughts with "harmony," "peace," and "resolution." If you want to get along with your co-workers, think about what it feels like to get along with them. If you want a happy relationship, think about a healthy relationship. If you want to see the demise of destructive natural disasters, stop thinking destructively. Stop thinking about how you're going to fight with your enemies and start thinking about how it would be to have a loving relationship with them. The one true way to conquer any kind of nemesis is to feed them love. Blast love out into the Universal group consciousness. Create your own peaceful world and you'll begin to slowly see peace roll up hill.

Every civilization and culture likes to dictate to the other civilizations and cultures how to live their lives. It's the source of many a war and conflict. In this unilateral narcissistic world, everyone wants his or her own way. Be the first on your block to not need it all your own way, and you'll see immediate change. Stop believing that your happiness is dictated by how many times you're right and how often you get your own way. Yes, it's perfectly natural to want things, but you have to remember you're not the only one on your block. Open up to the idea that the space you're in is shared. You are part of a Universal society and as such, the space belongs to all of us. Know that and be respectful and respect will come back to you. As long as you keep drawing lines in the sand to get what you want you will always have something to fight about. Wipe away the lines in the sand and instead build a castle everyone can enjoy.

I'll give you some things you can do to further help diminish the mad, mad, mad world. Notice I said diminish, not eradicate. While it sounds pessimistic, the reality is that there will probably never be complete peace on earth because we're all here for emotional knowledge. Emotional knowledge is achieved when you fix something that is amiss in your life. As you are in this body to gain emotional knowledge, you will live in a world where there will be conflict. Yet, the more you strive for peace, on scales small and large, you will take another step toward completing your quest for emotional knowledge, while making it as good as possible here on earth.

Take these simple steps to do your part in creating a more peaceful world.

1. Stop watching the news

If you want to get information about what is going on in the world, find a non-biased magazine like "The Economist" to read. Remember that visual media is meant to be just that: visual. Showing peace and good will does not sell the news. If it bleeds, it leads! Broadcast news is about scaring you. When you are trying to heal your soul and your environment, stop watching the news.

2. Pay attention

In order to participate in creating a more peaceful planet, you must pay attention to your life and how you feel about it. Also, pay attention to how you think and feel about others. Whenever you're fighting with someone, stop thinking about the fights and feel and see yourself resolving the issue. Stop thinking about how bad it is and think about how good it will turn out. Stop stirring the negative emotional pot and start seasoning it with kindness and love.

3. Meditate/visualize world peace

This is a simple idea. Either before you go to work or after you return, spend just five minutes visualizing a perfect, peaceful environment. Do it for every environment in which you find yourself – your home, work place, garden club, baseball game, and yes, even do it for the global community. A few minutes of your time is little to ask to help create world peace. A few minutes of peaceful visualization will change your world and in turn, the world around you. You have the potential and responsibility to make the world as glorious as it can possibly be. You can either add to the chaos or help prevent it.

13
SPIRITS AND DEMONS

Often times you become f'd up because of the unknown forces of the other side. The "other side" is an energy vibration that is different from the energy vibration of the earth plane. You can be adversely affected by these entities. To further explain, it would help to understand the differences between the disembodied spirits or the dead people that can adversely affect your world.

Ghosts: A *ghost* is said to be the apparition of someone deceased, frequently similar in appearance to when they were alive. Ghosts are usually encountered in places she or he frequented, like the place of his or her death, or in association with their former worldly belongings.

Disincarnated spirits: A *disincarnate spirit* may be one that acts as a spiritual counselor or protector to a living, incarnated human being. They may also be spirits that actually mean no harm to their living friend, or the inhabitants of a home, but they want to stick around to watch or help a home, business owner, or person. They can also be spirits that attach themselves to you because they feel you can help them in some way.

Demons: A *demon* is a supernatural being that is often described as a malevolent spirit. Demons are often much more difficult to remove than ghosts because of their desire to overtake and inhabit a living, breathing human being's body.

Each of these three entity types is made up of all dead people, but their effects range from annoying to possessing. Depending on their level of vibration, their presence can run the gamut from irritating to overpowering. These dead people can control your disposition, make you do things that you normally would not do, or just plain scare the hell out of you.

Ghosts usually just want to get your attention. Because they usually attach themselves to buildings, they are easier to remove. If they have died in the house you now inhabit, they might just want you out. For the most part, ghosts are just as afraid of you as you are of them. They can move objects or turn lights off and on, but the purpose is usually just to get your attention. These Casper-like ghosts usually mean no harm. They are not trying to harm you, just contact you.

Some ghosts don't realize they're dead. They just know they're suffering and they need help. These lost souls attach themselves to you so that you can help them to either move on or understand their own pain. Negative spirits sometimes attach themselves to living, breathing people because they feel camaraderie with them. Sometimes that camaraderie stems from an old wound they see in you that coincides with an old wound of theirs. Because disincarnated spirits are able to see your energy, if you are angry, guilty, or depressed and they are angry, guilty, or depressed, they will attach themselves to you. Birds of a feather do indeed flock together. They desperately want someone to hear them and relate to them so they choose kindred spirits. They may sense that you are sensitive to their existence and hope you can help them. If they did drugs when they were alive, they will attach themselves to a drug user because they believe they are buddies just hanging out together. They think you know they are there and are just partying with you. Just like with living, breathing humans, like attracts like. If these spirits see that you're in the same pain they were in when they were in the body, they will attach themselves to you. What this does is enhance your already existing negative emotions. Your pain will increase, and if you were already doing drugs, you will uncontrollably do more. These spirits don't realize they are harming you; they are just trying to relate to you.

Demons are the darker entities that want to attach to you in order to possess your body. Scary, I know – the idea that your inner demons are not necessarily always your own. More frightening is the fact that the source of a great deal of evil in this world is from these possessions. These unloving beings attach themselves to human beings with the intention of systematically taking over their souls and their lives; i.e. possession. They can and do control your mind, thereby causing you to believe that their thoughts are yours. They can make you drink when you normally don't want to, they can make you over-eat, they can make you angry with other people, and they can even convince the very weak-minded to commit heinous crimes, like murder. While it may seem far-fetched, I have witnessed first-hand the results of someone possessed by dark, evil entities. These stories might be a little too graphic to share, but have you ever watched *The Exorcist*? That film was based on the true-life events of a little boy in St. Louis. How about *The Exorcism of Emily Rose*? Both of these were based on actual events that depicted evil, disincarnated spirits possessing humans, and then systematically destroying their lives. If you are a victim of a possession you will usually need to get some professional help to exorcise the demon. It's difficult to do on your own. Possession is the worst-case scenario of spirit attachment; however, most cases are less intense, so much so that most of the time you don't realize it's happening. With possession, the spirit is literally in control of your actions and thoughts by literally overtaking your weakened soul. Possession means you lose yourself in their power. Spirit attachment means they are energetically so close to you that they can and often do influence your decisions. Most cases are simply spirit attachment and not possession.

What does spirit attachment feel like? Imagine going to a party and having some crazy character follow you home. Imagine this character was a drug addict who abused cocaine. Imagine this character became your houseguest and you were around their destructive behavior all the time. Eventually you might begin to empathize with them. Eventually you might begin to engage in the destructive behavior with them. Have you ever had a friend that drank more than you did and the more time you spent with him or her, the more you drank? Now imagine that's happening to you, but there isn't a friend; there isn't anyone around that you can physically see enticing you to engage in these behaviors. That's how it is with negative spirit attachment. They have the ability to influence your life with their negative energy.

Not all spirits that attach themselves to humans are dark entities with evil intentions. Most dark spirits will only trouble themselves with weak-minded, low-vibrational people. It's easier for them – kind of like a thief will most often choose to rob the house with the open window. Some spirits are merely seeking help, and if you are normally sensitive to the energies of others, you are probably a good candidate for frequent spirit attachments. I have a friend who picks up a spirit several times a month. Why do they follow her so much? She's a light being and they know it, so they attach themselves to her, hoping she'll recognize them and help them. She's become better over the years at identifying them before they adversely affect her life. She seldom attracts demonic spirits as she's raised her vibration to a level that doesn't attract them.

A negative spirit has the same influence on you as a negative family member or friend might, only worse, because you can't see them. The family member with dark energy that drinks too much or says hurtful things to you can destroy your happiness. The negative spirit that attaches to you and is with you twenty-four hours a day can destroy your life. I've worked with many clients with attachments and they often have no idea they're there or why their lives are such a disaster. One such client called in a panic because she hadn't eaten or slept in three days. She needed me to come see her. When I arrived at her house, I was shocked to see what a mess she was. She was as wired as if she'd been on a cocaine binge, except she hadn't done any drugs. She'd lost six pounds and her nose was as red as if she had been doing lines for a week. She hadn't. Fortunately, I was able to talk to the young female spirit that had attached to her. It was a twenty-five-year-old woman who had died of a cocaine overdose, but wasn't aware she'd died. She attached herself to my client, thinking she would be a friend who could help her find more drugs so they could do them together. The reason she chose my client was because my client had been a drug user in the past and had yet to completely heal those old wounds. Naturally, because of this history and the spirit attachment, my client was terrified but had no idea what was wrong. Within minutes of my removing the spirit from her energy system, she returned to her normal, healthy self.

On an episode of Oprah, a man was featured who had

been so depressed he stabbed his twin five-year-old girls to death. He said he heard voices in his head telling him there was no hope for a positive future for his children so he should kill them in order to free them. What happened to this seemingly normal, loving father that would cause him to commit such a heinous act? I believe it was a demonic possession. I believe the demon started to control his subconscious mind by influencing his thoughts. This demon continually told the man that his children's lives were in danger, so to save them he must kill them. After hearing those thoughts over time he began to believe they were his own thoughts. The powerful demon took away his ability to think. He took away his ability to reason. The demon's energy was more powerful than the father's mind. He lost himself to this demon. Over time, the demon's thoughts became the father's thoughts. He allowed his thoughts to be infiltrated by the mind of a depressed spirit to the extent that it convinced him that killing his children was the logical thing to do. Other people believe this man was evil; I believe the spirit was. The man was weak and the spirit was strong. That doesn't mean the father should not be punished; it only explains why he did it.

Knowing that negative spirits exist is the first step in protecting yourself from their attachment. The more you know about their existence and their potential for attachment, the better chance you have of not attracting one. The more attention you pay to your feelings and thoughts, the better protected you are. If you know yourself really well, you will know when another entity is attempting to attach itself to you. Do you ever hear yourself say; "I just don't feel like myself today?" That's one of the first signs that you probably aren't yourself but are being adversely affected by a spirit. If you start feeling uncharacteristically angry, you will know something outside of yourself is affecting your behavior. If for no apparent reason, you are having an overly difficult emotional day, pay attention to what your feelings are and what feelings might be coming from an outside source. You can consciously overcome any attachment. Don't be afraid of them, as fear gives them power. Simply pay attention, acknowledge that they're there, and then with loving thoughts, send them on their way. Remember these negative spirits are no different than the rest of us; they had painful experiences that caused painful wounds. The only difference is that they didn't heal these wounds before they died.

Healing what you don't see

How does one go about protecting themselves from what they can't see?

> 1. Pay attention and protect
> Are you noticing a trend here? Pay attention to what is going on with you. If you are paying attention to your own thoughts and actions, you will know when another entity's thoughts and actions are adversely influencing yours. If you are having a bad day, stop and pay attention to why you're having a bad day. Pay attention to any feeling or thought that seems random. Are you behaving uncharacteristically? That is the key word to recognizing spirit attachment. Uncharacteristic. If you don't feel like yourself, you probably aren't.
>
> Pay attention when you are in a situation that might normally be a haven for dark entities. Bars, for example, are smorgasbords for spirits – literally. These places are Disneyland for demons looking for kindred spirits. Protect your heart and energy before entering one by surrounding yourself with

the pure white light of love. Surround yourself with love by thinking of something that makes you joyous, be it your pet's antics, a loved one's smile, or the last beautiful sunset you enjoyed. Imagine wrapping yourself in Saran Wrap to protect your energy system and shield it from darkness. Do this *before* you go anywhere! If you already have another ritual of protection, use it. It doesn't matter how you fill yourself with divine love – it just matters that you do it.

2. You're the one with the body; be in charge!
Let's say that you're doing a good job of paying attention and you notice you're having adverse, unhealthy random thoughts. You've noticed you're uncharacteristically angry with your lover; everything they do irritates you, so now is the time to take charge. Tell the spirit to go away. Light some candles; put on some peaceful music and have a conversation with the spirit. Be firm, but loving and tell the spirit to move along. Literally say out loud, "Go away. I cannot help you. Go away. You're not wanted here. Go away. God bless you." If you don't feel any different, then make a stronger command. Here's a good mantra to say when you don't feel like you can send the negative attachment away:

I am surrounded by the pure white light of the Christ.
Only good can come to me, only good can come from me.
I bless you and send you to your highest good.

Repeat this mantra until you feel the energy lift away from you. Use this mantra any time you don't feel like yourself. As soon as you recognize you're not acting like yourself, take charge of your body and your life.

3. Cleanse your energy

You need a weekly ritual to cleanse your energy system from unwanted attachments. One night a week, shut down your energy and cleanse by taking a ritualistic *soul bath*. The following is a recipe for the soul bath I've been taking for years. This ritual will help keep your energy system clean and free of spirits and will also bring you peace of mind:

    a. Turn off all electronic devices, including your computer, radio or CD player. No music is needed.
    b. Shut off all phones. Yes, this means your cell. No calls or text messages.
    c. Light as many white candles as possible, as well as incense.
    d. Light a stick of sage and wave it around your home and body.
    e. Immerse yourself in a sea salt and baking soda bath for about twenty minutes.
    f. Think of things that bring joy, such as loved ones, pets, friends, and laughter. Get out of the tub.
    g. Lie down on your bed.
    h. Meditate by focusing on one thing, such as a lit candle. Or better yet, focus on nothing.
    i. Following your meditation, get a notepad and write down where your mind went. What were you thinking about as you tried to meditate?
    j. With pen in hand, ask God one question.

For example: "God, what is the emotional block that is keeping me from being in a relationship?" Then without thinking, just start writing. Write down what you think is the answer and then write down whatever you are hearing in your head. This is automatic writing. You'll get better and better the more you do it. You'll start hearing answers. After all, you are divine knowledge and you have all the answers if you take the time to listen to yourself.

k. Once again, close your eyes. Say, "I love me" at least twenty-five times. Give yourself a big hug.

l. Go to sleep in peace.

14
SPIRITUAL GROWTH AIN'T EASY

I know that I work on my soul more than the average person; I am constantly paying attention to my reactions. I notice when my chest tightens up, my head hurts, or I get sick to my stomach. I pay attention when I feel any negative emotion whether it is sadness, anger, loneliness, or frustration. Yet, with all this mental and emotional work, I, like everyone else, still have painful experiences. The difference now, as opposed to when I didn't pay attention, is that I try to embrace those reactions, rather than judge them.

Your soul is set on automatic pilot to evolve. As you delve into the depths of your soul, you continually open up more and more. You falsely believe that the goal is to have absolute peace. You believe that once you tackle the really big emotional issues the rest should be easy. The more spiritual awareness you acquire, the more intense the pain. The more aware your soul becomes, the more you cannot go against one ounce of your truth without experiencing the repercussions from it. The purer the soul, the more narrow the path of truth.

Pema Chodron, an American Buddhist nun, wrote in *When Things Fall Apart* that embarking on the spiritual journey is like getting into a very small boat and setting out on the ocean to search for unknown lands. I would add that the boat is always rocking. There's just no way to avoid it. You can't possibly have spiritual growth without some choppy waters and fear of them – fear that must be faced and conquered. "Fear," Pema wrote, "is a natural reaction to moving closer to the truth" (page 1). Inside of you are a bundle of memories that will either be dealt with or buried deeper depending on your reactions to them. If you're afraid to feel anything but love, then you will never get to the core issues of your soul. You are an inhabitant of this earthly experiment to feel! Feeling bad as well as good is imperative to your success.

Humans mistakenly think that if they're feeling bad, something is wrong; however, feeling bad is the first indicator that you're growing, that you're alive. Why be afraid of something that makes you feel alive? Why fear something that helps you grow? No one goes through life unscathed. We are all dealt difficult hands. Life is all about how you play the cards you're dealt. In order to get through these situations, you have to look the pain straight in the eye and ask, "What are you trying to tell me? What is the lesson here?" When you're afraid in these situations, you need to ask the fear what is it that you are being protected from? Find the fear, face the fear, and you can change what could be lifelong twinges of fear into brief passing moments.

As you get into this game of life and begin to grow spiritually, your soul starts to open up and reveal more painful memories – and that's when it can get messy. You're designed to remember the pain so you can heal the pain.

The more you open to your truth, the more truth is revealed to you and with it comes the pain of spiritual growth. You have layers and layers of wounds that need to be uncovered. Sometimes it feels as if you will never have peace because you will never get to the bottom of the wounds. That's the whole point of incarnating – to get to the bottom of the wounds – but it doesn't mean you will get to them all. Spiritual growth exacerbates spiritual growth. The more you grow, the more your soul wants to grow. It often feels like it'd be nice to take a break from growth, because sometimes it is so exhausting. As you get deeper into the layers the intensity of the pain is deeper, but the time it takes to heal is shorter. Hang in there. The growth is more intense, but it lasts a shorter period of time.

The good or bad news – depending upon your perspective – is that whether or not you open up to spiritual awareness, you will still experience spiritual growth. You then have the choice to either embrace the true pleasure and appreciation of your soul moving forward or to ignore it. Whether you become conscious of your soul's growth or not will not change the fact your soul will continue to grow. It will release the painful memories of the past whether or not you are aware of or in command of them. Being aware makes the experience a temporary, controlled one, instead of a mysterious one that lasts a lifetime.

You can never walk away from spiritual growth. You can never hide from it, no matter how messy or uncomfortable it appears to be. Like death and taxes, it will always be there. You can either play the game with blindfolds on or master the game with your eyes wide open. Of course, if you have blindfolds on, you'll miss the opportunity for awareness. You choose. As you make that choice, though, consider that the greatest benefit of getting into and mastering the game is that the pain passes much more quickly and leaves you filled with the joy and pride of growing.

As I've stated earlier, the ugly lawsuit I was involved in forced me to grow in ways I'd never imagined. I had always believed people could talk and fix any situation diplomatically and with kindness, yet suddenly I found myself in a situation that required me to litigate. The other side got lawyers, so I was forced to do the same. Without getting into details I can tell you this was the most significant fear-facing situation of my life. My soul had a very adverse reaction to the lawyers for the defense. I'd never experienced a karmic situation as powerful as the one I had when facing the lawyers in my depositions. I was terrified of them. I almost had a nervous breakdown after the last of the three depositions. I was paranoid, found myself walking the streets at 4 a.m., terrified of what I had said at my deposition. I was scared to death that I had said something that they could use against me in trial. I was no longer my strong, powerful self. My reactions made no sense to my family and friends, who knew me as a very strong, confident, and capable woman. I was terrified to the point of literally being brought to my knees. I meditated, trying to find peace. I intuitively looked for the reason behind my unrealistic reaction. I had psychic friends trying to look at the reaction as well. It seemed beyond my control. I was having an unrealistic reaction to the karma. In many lifetimes, these same lawyers had been my persecutors, causing my death; so, when I faced them for the third time, my soul had a cellular reaction. My soul didn't recognize the difference in space and time; rather, all it recognized was persecution and death. The fear of death was so horrific that I believed in this lifetime they were going to destroy me.

They don't exactly hang you from the rafters these days in real estate litigation, so I knew on a cerebral level that my reactions were illogical; yet my fear was grounded in my personal soul history. I continued to pray and meditate to convince my subconscious mind to release the fear, to convince my subconscious mind I was not in danger of dying; that this was a very different lifetime. Even though I found the source of the reaction, I couldn't stop it. Eventually, I was able to get into the game, master it, overcome my fear, and finally put lifetimes of persecution and death behind me. Because of that horrific experience, I am finally free of that karma of persecution. Once I was able to face the karmic perpetrators and not die, my subconscious realized I was not only safe, but also safe to advance in other areas of my life.

My past life experiences with persecution were holding me back in this lifetime from pursuing my dreams. Unwittingly, these same situations held me back because my subconscious was protecting me from achieving my dreams in this lifetime. My fears prevented me from writing books, giving lectures, and ultimately becoming recognized. My subconscious was protecting me out of the fear that putting myself and my views out there would once again cause me to be persecuted and killed. Since those depositions and that experience, I am free of the fear of persecution. I go out into the world every day, exposing my truth and myself. I am no longer afraid of people gossiping, insulting, or ridiculing me – current equivalents of my past life persecution. When you worry about what others think of you, try to remember Jesus. He was a near-perfect being yet they crucified him. Just know that no matter what you do, someone won't like it. Someone will judge you because they are really only judging themselves.

I have made great strides with my career, thanks to the painful growth experience of the lawsuit. I know I would not be on the precipice of achieving my hopes and dreams were it not for being forced to get in the game and face my fear. That spiritual growth wasn't easy, but now I am truly grateful for it.

15
GET IN THE GAME

Several times throughout this book I have mentioned that in order to heal you must first *get in the game*. Getting in the game means to become aware of the fact that you are presumably f'd up and why. This is not limited to personal experiences either. You must also be aware of and have an understanding of others and the fact they are just as f'd up as you. You must pay attention to the dark forces of the world as much as the light. You must realize there's something inside of you that wants to heal. You must realize that the external world is a reflection of your internal world and your life experiences are designed to help you see inside your soul. You manifest into your life the experiences that will help your inherent wounds to surface and so, whenever you need to grow, you manifest the wounds and circumstances to bring them to light. When you get in the game, you will stop struggling over why your life is so screwed up and start recognizing there's a reason behind it. You will also recognize you are not alone and every living person is going through the exact same thing, just in different scenarios.

We are all in this together and whether you realize it or not, we all help each other. Our physical world was designed to awaken to our individual as well as global connections. The illusion you call life has a greater purpose than most people can possibly fathom. It is only by looking through the eyes and heart of the creator that it's possible to comprehend what is really going on in the world.

If you do not take a spiritual approach to life, you will not be able to understand the ugly parts of it; you will always have the perspective that the world is f'd up. If you look at life purely from a surface perspective, it will always appear to be in chaos. If you change your perspective, you will find f'd up truly is a state of mind and you can change your state any time you're ready and willing.

The dark forces in the world will help you see the light in your world, if you will give them the opportunity. You can't know who you are until you know who you're not. Can any of you even fathom understanding the likes of Hitler or Jeffrey Dahmer, or even excuse what they did? Absolutely not, yet there is a purpose for evil as well as for good. It's what you do with the evil that matters. Can you understand the perpetrators of evil? Can you look past their actions and into their wounded souls? Admittedly, it's harder to look past the actions of the truly evil, but you can start by looking past the unhealthy actions of those you love. You can embrace the poor souls who drink too much, who stick needles in their arms, who become thieves, or those who hurt us with their words and deeds. You can show compassion by knowing they have pain as you have pain. You don't have to excuse their actions, but you have to understand them. Don't try to heal them--you have enough on your hands with yourself--just send them loving kindness.

Compassion brings people closer together. Compassion for self opens up your heart for compassion for others. When you begin by feeling compassion for those closest to you, you begin to feel compassion for those you don't know, for those whose actions may be deplorable. Their actions themselves do not dictate that you feel compassion, yet the more horrific the act, the more horrific the pain. I am not saying you should ignore the horrific acts or that the perpetrators should not be punished, but you need to have love and understanding in your heart. You need to feel sympathetic to the darkness they reveal to you. You need to stop thinking of them in an unloving manner and start thinking of them in the loving manner that God thinks of you. If you truly desire them to rehabilitate, then you must view them as God would. In thinking about crimes, you must send loving benevolence to those who commit the crimes. With empathy, you will use their evil to raise your consciousness and the consciousness around you. By hating, you create more hate; by loving, you have more love and caring in your own life. By empathizing with others, you will feel gratitude for your life and that gratitude will affect those around you.

Getting in the game means that you pay attention to what's going on around you with understanding, rather than judgment. Pay attention in order to understand the pain others are suffering, which will help you understand why you are suffering. You can use the darkness, sadness, and anger of others to help you forgive your own darkness, sadness, and anger. Paying attention to the emotions that are evoked by the negative actions of others will help you see your own more clearly. With a new perspective about the truth of this world, you will stop being f'd up.

Being on a spiritual path does not make you closer to God than anyone else. You can read every book ever written on spiritual enlightenment, but until you start to recognize the purpose of pain in your life, you won't grow any closer to your truth; and that is the truth that counts. Just because you've read something and are able to espouse your knowledge to friends doesn't make you enlightened. You have to walk the walk, not just talk the talk. *Knowing* something and *being* something are two very separate truths. You may know that you're not supposed to gossip about others, but actually *not* gossiping when among others that do is living your truth. Walking away from the situation and sending love to the person in question is living the truth. We are all one, so when you gossip and it hurts them, you're only hurting yourself.

So often I hear people say they aren't religious, they're spiritual. That's become a catch phrase for many who want to believe in God or a higher power and yet don't choose to associate with any religious organization. There are people who go to church every Sunday, but as soon as the service is over they behave badly. My father would never miss a sermon Sunday morning or beating up his children Sunday afternoon. Attending a service doesn't mean a person is on the right path. There are people who attend church who are wonderful, giving human beings and kind to everyone they meet. There are also people who study every spiritual book they can find, but still judge everything and everyone around them. They live their lives as if they haven't understood a word they've read. The earth plane was designed to be a spiritual path, so everyone here is on a spiritual path; they're just moving along it at different paces.

You may not like the game of life that others are playing, but you must recognize that it is their game. We are all spiritual! Whether you attend church every Sunday or read books by the Dalai Lama, you are on a path. If you rob, steal, or even harm another person, you are on a path; you're just on a negative one. Being on a spiritual path means being. As a spiritual being you choose how you discover yourself. Whether you discover your inner wounds by being involved in organized religion, following a guru, or taking long walks and meditating, you are on a spiritual path. You manifest events, people and lifestyles that help you reveal your pain, and as you read earlier, discovering your pain is how you become aware and *get in the game*!

Have you ever heard the expression, "You're projecting?" Well, you project your own worries and fears onto your loved ones. Whenever you're having a difficult time with an aspect of yourself, you will manifest someone into your life to help you see that aspect of yourself. You will manifest a selfish person into your life when you need to work on your own selfish behavior. The mirror effect was designed because it's easier to see what needs to be changed in you when you see it in others. How do you recognize when you're projecting? When another person's actions or emotions bother you. Anytime someone does something that annoys you to the point of disrupting your peaceful flow of life, you become angry and irritated; then you are projecting an aspect of yourself onto them. I'm sure you'd like to believe that some people just do annoying things, and I'm not saying they don't; but if you find yourself getting overly emotional about their actions, you must look at your own actions. It's like the old saying, "If you're pointing your finger at someone else, you have three fingers pointing back at you." To get in the game you must notice whenever someone irritates you and try and figure out why his or her actions bother you so much. When you figure out that annoying aspect of yourself that you see so clearly in others, you can heal that aspect of yourself.

When you realize and understand humans are all playing this game of life together, you will have a new reality. Everyone is hurting and helping each other discover who they really are. Humans run the gamut from revolting to inspiring. As a whole we represent every single aspect of God. If you dissect the human race, taking a good long look, without judgment, you will discover a world filled with every thought and emotion possible. Some of your friends are jealous, some focus on the physical, some are narcissistic, some are selfish, some judgmental, some loving, some sarcastic, some sweet, some generous, and so on and so on. These are all aspects of God. Every possible aspect of God is played out in the human experience. That truth is part of the game you are playing.

Join in the awareness – *get in the game*!

16
CONCLUSION

Now that you've read the entire book, I hope you've come to the realization that contrary to the title, you are not actually F'd Up – you only appear to be! The truth is that the world you live in is an illusion. Your personal life may be in chaos, but the reality is that you are being provided an opportunity to heal old karmic wounds, so the chaos is divinely planned. The most important thing to remember is that the soul knows no space and no time. As far as it's concerned, it's all happening at the same time, so the chaos you experience today is directly related to chaos of the past. In order to put an end to this chaos once and for all, you need to find the source of it--whether it's in this lifetime or another--and with diligence and compassion fix it.

The key to unlocking the doorway into a healthy, happy life is to *get into the game*. Always be aware that there is something much bigger going on than what meets your limited consciousness. Opening your mind to the opportunities that pain gives you expands your consciousness to the possibilities of healing. When you do that, you discover the root of your suffering. Through this discovery you learn why you are having problems in your relationships, and how your current pain relates to that in your childhood. All you need to do to end the pain is to become aware of the "why." Once you do and become aware that life is all about healing opportunities, your perspective of life will completely change and you will find yourself living in joy.

How you picture your life determines whether you live in joy or sorrow. Happiness is all about perspective. If you believe in a God that punishes you when you make a mistake, you will believe you need to be punished when you make a mistake. You will believe you need to suffer if you believe in a divine being that believes you should suffer. God does not need to punish you because of the way the human experience was designed. Karmic justice always prevails and your soul will always want to experience every negative moment you inflict on others. So, even if you do screw up in this lifetime, the Universe will give you an opportunity to fix it – be it in this lifetime or another. God understands that screwing up gives you tremendous opportunities for growth and rejoices in those growth opportunities. He/she has nothing but love for you when you harm yourself and others; so you, too, should have mercy. Embrace God's perspective and you will never feel lost or ashamed.

A proper perspective on sex and relationships is difficult, but must be maintained if you want to mend your wounded spirit. If you have the wrong perspective, the truth becomes convoluted and you become unhappy. Good sex can cause you to stay in an otherwise unhealthy relationship if your perspective is that good sex means you have something infinitely special. In reality, sex was designed as a healing mechanism for humans, to be a connection to your truth and love. It was designed to bring your soul together with another in order to feel real love, yet a good sexual relationship will *not* guarantee a long-term relationship. A powerful sexual connection is all about karma, *not* about good sex, and is never a reason to stay in a relationship. Doing so will only delay your growth. Kindness, consideration, similarity of interests, friendship, honesty, and caring are the characteristics of a good, healthy relationship. Don't worry – sex is in there too, but you should never allow it to be the focal point.

Perspective on religion is a large cause for people being emotionally and mentally f'd up. Your religious beliefs should make you happy, not unhappy, and they should never infringe upon another's. Everyone in the world should be allowed to worship in the way they see fit as long as it does not intrude on another's choice of worship. Your perspective about religion should be the same as God's: to each his own. If being a Baptist or a Catholic makes you a happier, nicer person, then by all means, be a Baptist or a Catholic. If being a Buddhist keeps you calm, then be a Buddhist. Just remember that it is your choice as it is the choice of everyone else. Don't allow yourself to tell others their choices are wrong and don't let others' choices or religious beliefs make you unhappy. You want to believe what you want to believe, so give them the same respect – otherwise you're being hypocritical.

The basics

If your life seems f'd up, there's a mental or emotional reason for it. Your inner child, your subconscious protector, karma, destructive thoughts, group consciousness, spirit attachment, ignoring pain, and spiritual growth can all be causes of your misery. In order to heal, you must *pay attention*.

When your life is in turmoil you need to stop ignoring it. You need to stop and figure out which of the above reasons is causing you to be f'd up. Look at the thoughts you have about life, look at your perspective on things, and look back at your childhood to see if you have old wounds that keep popping up. Stop ignoring your pain and embrace it. Don't judge it. Step back and observe it with loving-kindness. Delve into why things aren't going as well as you'd like them to. Find the root cause of the pain by seeking out old wounds that need healing. Innately your soul needs to heal, so pain will always surface in order to do it.

Be aware that all physical, mental, and emotional reactions you have are indicative of an internal pain. When the body is sick the soul is talking. Every disease we have starts in the soul. Life is an emotional game, so play it by not letting your emotions play with you.

So, to answer your question, the one that prompted you to pick up this book, "Why am I F'd Up?": it's because you're supposed to be! So take a moment, take it in, embrace it, and get in the game. Your soul will thank you for it.

17
MY STORY

Now that you've read *Why am I F'd Up*? I want to explain who I am. So often we believe that authors are experts simply because they've written a book. Writing a book should not necessarily qualify you as an expert, so I wanted to let you know why I feel qualified to have written it.

In our country, the only education that seems to be recognized is college (university), and life experience is discredited in many fields. If I were going in for heart surgery, I'd want the most educated surgeon opening my chest; yet as far as spirituality is concerned, there is no college experience that can possibly give you the education you need. Life gives you that education. Experience, practice, and hands-on training give you the knowledge you need to be able to successfully teach others about their spiritual selves. I've had plenty of practice. A man once asked me who taught me to do what I do. I simply told him the truth … God. There is no one in this world that can teach you what God can teach you. God was and is my professor.

I've been working professionally as an empathic

intuitive, spirit medium, psychic, and past-life therapist for over eighteen years. I was born with the ability to see and hear spirits. To me, listening to spirit guides or speaking with those that have passed on to the other side is as easy as pie. I've always been able to do it. As the years passed, I learned to "see" intuitively into a person's body to help them understand what their subconscious mind was thinking. An empathic intuitive is a person that has the ability to speak with your internal energy system. Basically, I talk to the conscious, subconscious, and higher conscious minds simultaneously. Unlike a regular intuitive, I literally feel the pain of others. Then, I tune into your soul to find out not only what's wrong, but also the source of it. I help clients understand the *why* behind their destructive treatment of themselves and others.

One would think the ability to contact those on the other side would be something to be cherished, but for years I desperately tried to ignore it. I was terrified of being able to see dead people. I was terrified because I was told that I was hearing the voice of the devil. As mentioned earlier, my father was a Baptist minister, and he taught me that if you were a girl and you heard voices, you must have been talking to the devil. He told me that the devil has the ability to disguise himself as anyone, so it was he I saw, not a benevolent spirit or angel. I was taught that only men of the church could speak with God, and that God did not give messages to any women, especially little girls. So, anytime I told my family I was talking to someone *without a body* they would tell me it was the devil and I shouldn't listen. That's what I did; I tried hard to ignore the voices in my head. As I grew up I was so afraid of the devil taking over my body that I started drinking and subsequently became an alcoholic. I was drinking my gift away, because I didn't know it was a gift. The last thing I wanted was to see and hear spirits.

Alcohol took the voices away. I just wanted the devil to leave me alone.

Thanks to the negative experiences of my childhood I became an explorer. Regardless of all that had happened and as much as I tried to avoid it, I couldn't fight my true nature. I had an inherent need to learn about other religions than the one in which I'd been raised. Christianity made no sense to me. It seemed that they believed God was intolerant and would punish you whenever he felt like it. I argued with my family about what I considered to be the ridiculous nature of this religion. My father refused to engage in discourse, choosing instead to be incensed that a girl would think she could know God better than him. Ironically, had it not been for the fact that my father was a Baptist minister who beat me; I would never have sought out God. His cruelty made me a seeker of the true God. My God is kind, understanding, loving, and funny. My God does not need to forgive me because my God does not ever think I make mistakes. My God knows my so-called mistakes are just learning opportunities. God loves you no matter what you do and realizes that when you hurt others, you do so because you do not love yourself enough. That's the God I found because of the un-God-like actions of my family. My father's cruelty became a true blessing. If not for his distorted beliefs I would not have the understanding of God that I have today.

Earlier in the book, I mentioned Sandy, the fellow broadcasting student with whom I took a road trip for a job. I mentioned her referral to the spiritual healer that helped me identify the past-life pain that was keeping me from my present-life's true path. It was after this healer, Lana, helped me that I decided I needed to learn how to do what she did. I decided I wanted to be able to help other people the way she helped me. I took classes from her where I learned about spirit guides, channeling, and meditation. I read every book I could about anything spiritual. I began meditating for an hour and a half a day without fail. From Shirley MacLaine to Ruth Montgomery, I wanted to know everything there was to know about the soul. I was addicted to my spiritual education. Other than my daughter, it was all I cared about. It literally changed my life.

My meditation practice became increasingly more intense. I was able to spend time in total and complete silence. I taught myself to let go of all thoughts. My meditations were not designed to see God, but to see nothing. I wanted to be able to release all thoughts so that I could then hear my spirit guides. It worked. I began receiving intuitive messages and as I continued with my meditations, my intuitive abilities rapidly increased. I didn't know how I knew; I just knew I knew things about people I couldn't possibly have known without intuition. I practiced tuning into friends to see what I could find out for them. It was fun. Little by little I began to perfect my gift of speaking with spirits.

I'll never forget the day I first actually felt a spirit. I'd been frustrated by the fact that I could hear them, but couldn't feel or see them. I was living in a house with a basement family room that also served as a laundry room. I needed to run downstairs to put a load into the dryer and as I rounded a corner, I hit an energy field that literally knocked me back a foot. It scared the daylights out of me. I screamed bloody murder. My partner at the time ran down the stairs, terrified of what might have happened. When I told him I'd finally *run* into a spirit, he laughed, saying from now on I should be careful what I wished for.

In the beginning, I accepted donations for my work. I didn't want to take money, but felt I had to or no one would value what I did. I had a full-time job, so I could only do readings on weekends. It limited me, but was enough so I could continue to improve my skills. Doing those readings helped me become more proficient in trusting my intuition, which is key to speaking with the other side. You have to trust the thoughts that you're having are ones being put there by spirit guides. When I do readings, I do not hear or see someone else's voice in my head; rather, it is my own voice giving me the words of the guides. After doing this for such a long time, I can tell the difference between the thoughts of others and my own. The more you can learn to trust your intuition, the more intuitive your life will be.

In 1998, I decided to devote myself full-time to spiritual teachings. I quit my job and dedicated my life to helping others and have been doing it as my job ever since. By working with clients and helping them with their problems, I've been able to understand some of my own. One would think that my life would be simple and easy because I do what I do, but it isn't. Like everyone else in the world, I'm a human being with karma and old wounds that need to be healed. I'm a psychic, not a saint.

My eighteen years of experience doing intuitive readings, past-life therapy, and spirit-medium work coupled with my own life experiences are what qualify me to write this book. I've dedicated my life to teaching others the truth behind their life difficulties; so writing this book is another way for me to teach. I hope that ***Why Am I F'd Up?*** gives you insight into the truth behind your suffering, as well as the truth behind the suffering in the world. My prayer is that this book will help every individual who reads it so that those individuals can help change the world.

Much love and God bless,

Pamela

www.ingramcontent.com/pod-product-compliance
Lightning Source LLC
Chambersburg PA
CBHW060829050426
42453CB00008B/629